D1395460

WHAT
THE ANIMALS
TELL ME

Sonya Fitzpatrick

with Patricia Burkhart Smith

WHAT
THE ANIMALS
TELL ME

The Secrets of Communicating with Your Pet

SIDGWICK & JACKSON

First published 1997 by Hyperion, New York

First published in Great Britain 1998 by Sidgwick & Jackson
an imprint of Macmillan Publishers Ltd
25 Eccleston Place, London SW1W 9NF
and Basingstoke

Associated companies throughout the world

ISBN 0 283 06321 1

1 3 5 7 9 8 6 4 2

A CIP catalogue record for this book is available from
the British Library.

Phototypeset by Intype, London Ltd
Printed by Mackays of Chatham plc, Chatham, Kent

To my beloved Rhodesian Ridgeback, Bella, for the joy and happiness she brought to our family over so many years and for her steadfast loyalty and devotion.

This is my thank you to all those who, directly or indirectly, have helped to make this book happen.

To my friend and co-author Patricia Burkhart Smith, whom I met in 1995, when she was editor of my local paper, the *Woodlands Villager*. I contacted her to see if she would like to collaborate with me in writing a book about my early life and my experiences in working with animals. She agreed and we would meet once a week. I would talk and Patricia would transcribe on to her laptop. We worked in this way over a two-year period and, as with most collaborative relationships, there were occasional intense moments of drama and we laughed and cried our way through the formative stresses of writing a book. I am deeply indebted to Pat for the professionalism and literary expertise she contributed and for her organizational skills in bringing the manuscript to a successful conclusion. I would also like to express my thanks and appreciation to her children Megan and Carter for their patience and understanding while we have been writing the book.

To my mother who has never let me down, for her love and understanding. To my daughter Emma for her love, support, companionship and help in my journey through life. To my sons Sean and Patrick for a unique relationship based on equality, frankness and honesty that transcends the normal mother/son bonds.

To my husband Fitz for his help in the care and rescue of lost, abandoned and unwanted animals and for his love and compassion in sharing our home with many of our furry friends.

To my dear friends Val and Tom Patrick who gave me the opportunity and help when I most needed it and who opened up their hearts and home to me; and to my dear friend Claire Rowland whose encouragement, love, friendship and understanding means so much to me.

To my friend Stacey Vornbrook and her delightful feline companions, Hubert and Leonard.

To my friend Sylvia in New York, and to Topaz and Bruce who were instrumental in putting me in contact with my literary agents, Lowenstein and Associates; and to Nancy Yost of Lowenstein and Associates. When I visited New York during a terrible snowstorm, Nancy valiantly accompanied me on a series of introductory visits to publishers. With Nancy leading the way, we walked through blizzards and fell into drifts and came through smiling and undaunted. Nancy is a wonderful lady and a great trooper.

To Salise Shuttlesworth whose work and dedication in running Special Pals, a shelter where no healthy animal is ever put down, is a source of inspiration to all animal lovers; and to my foster home parents, Lois, Paula, Carol and Ann, who have consistently and conscientiously worked so hard in finding suitable permanent homes for unwanted and abandoned animals.

To my guides, Rosy, Dr Thompson, John, Harry Edwards, Edgar Cacey and my spiritual mentor St Francis.

To my publishers, Laurie Abkemeier, Senior Editor at Hyperion, and Gordon Scott Wise, Senior Editor at Boxtree/Sidgwick & Jackson, Sarah Bennie, Helen Surman, Liz Davis, Deborah Adams, Laura Morris at Abner Stein.

Lastly, to all my clients and their animal children whom I have been privileged to meet and help. Working closely with them over the last few years has been a rewarding, ennobling and humbling experience which has changed the direction and purpose of my life forever, and I dedicate myself to the pursuit of causes that will result in the improvement and betterment of life for all animal species.

CONTENTS

How often does one hear from devoted animal lovers, 'I wish there was some way I could know what my pet is thinking and feeling.' Well, there is such a way, but most people do not understand that they can connect their own human mind energy to their animal's mind energy and communicate. They believe what many of us have been told from early childhood, that it's impossible to communicate with our pets on any meaningful level. People don't realize that there is something unseen that exists between humans and animals – a telepathic channel we can all access to communicate with the animals we love.

I was fortunate as a child to be fully tuned in to this channel. Talking to animals was as natural for me as breathing. In fact, because of a profound hearing loss in both my ears that doctors did not discover until I was almost eleven, it was actually easier for me to understand what animals were communicating to me telepathically than what humans were communicating to me verbally. It was only as I grew older that I began to realize not everyone could 'talk' to animals in this same way.

As I'll explain in Chapter 1, at the age of ten, a heartbreaking trauma made me cut off the telepathic communication I had always enjoyed with my animal friends.

Many years passed, and I was an adult when I redis-covered the ability to speak telepathically with animals as the result of a remarkable spiritual experience in the spring of 1994.

Soon I felt the door to the world of communication with our animal friends opening once again. At first it was a bit confusing for me, and difficult to understand that I had been chosen for this work. But as the weeks passed, I felt my awareness of animal communication steadily increasing. My lifelong love for animals had culminated in this special gift.

I now know I have been chosen to help animals, to educate people about the often cruel or thoughtless ways that animals are treated, and to enlighten them about what they can do to make life easier for their pets. I do this by talking to animals and finding out how they think and feel.

People often ask me how I 'talk' to animals, how I make myself understood, and how I manage to understand what they are saying back to me. The method I use, though perhaps not widely known, is neither complex nor mystical. I use my mind's energy, sometimes called telepathy, to communicate with animals, to discover what is worrying them, what they like or dislike, and what makes them happy.

If they are hurting or hungry, I feel those sensations in my own body. A pleasantly full sensation tells me the animal is being regularly fed, while gnawing hunger pangs tell me just the opposite. If the animal has an ear or bladder infection, or is stiff with arthritis, I feel the exact symptoms in the correlating parts of my own body.

Every living thing – plants, trees, animals, human beings – gives off energy, and it is this energy I tune in to with my mind to establish communication with animals. It is easier to communicate in this way with animals than with other humans because animals are receptive to telepathic transmissions, whereas most humans, through years of conditioning, are not.

Telepathic communication is a universal language that transcends boundaries of time, distance and species. Many people unwittingly use telepathic communication when they have come to know their animal very well. They may think of it as reading the animal's body language, but whatever they call it, telepathy is a higher form of communication which uses a completely different part of our brain than that which we use in our day-to-day lives; a part most of us rarely access. Humans know simply that their dog or cat responds to their spoken commands or whistles, never realizing they may be communicating with their pets on this higher telepathic plane.

Though animals communicate quite readily by telepathy, humans have to learn to relax enough to be receptive to this form of communication. With a degree of concentration, each of us is capable of connecting on the telepathic level with an animal we love. We can learn to exchange mind energy with our pets, transmitting pictures and information back and forth with astounding speed, as there is no time or space as we understand them on the telepathic level.

Humans rely on speaking for communication because that is what is easiest and most natural for us, so we tend to discount the notion there might be an alternative way to convey thoughts, ideas, information, emotions and feelings. But just because animals do not 'speak' with words as humans do does not mean they do not communicate. Animals communicate with pictures and feelings they transmit telepathically. You may not realize it, but we humans can and do communicate telepathically in that same way. Let me give you an example.

If I asked you to tell me, 'Where is the Statue of Liberty?' your first impression would be a picture in your mind. Your brain would create a detailed mental image of the statue and its environs almost instantaneously. In your mind (or imagination) you would be able to 'see' the torch held high in one hand, the spikes of Liberty's crown, and the surrounding water. At the same moment you were 'seeing' these things, you might feel a sense of amazement, or wonder how they built such a large statue.

You probably think this 'picture' and these 'thoughts' and 'feelings' exist only in your imagination, but in fact at the moment you imagine it, that same picture you see so clearly in your mind begins transmitting out telepathically from your energy. If your dog or cat is nearby, they will receive the picture and perhaps start wondering why you are thinking of a large statue. If you look at them now, you might even catch the look of puzzlement on their faces.

We regularly lay out our plans in our heads before we do anything. We dream, we think great thoughts, we hatch ideas, we play out scenes. All this mental activity is broadcast telepathically as we produce it. These pictures, plus the feelings and emotions that accompany them, are the basic building blocks of telepathic communication, just as words are the building blocks of spoken communication.

Many people are not aware they have the ability to communicate in another language because they believe that spoken language is sufficient to cover all their communication needs. But this other telepathic language is the language animals understand and if you can master it, even on a very elementary level, you will greatly increase your understanding of your pet's motivations, which in turn will lead to a closer and more satisfying relationship with your pet.

You are probably not conscious of creating pictures from your mind energy or thoughts, even though you may 'see' them in your mind or imagination while you are creating them. As soon as you 'see' the picture and verbally relate or explain whatever thoughts accompany that picture, your mind races on to its next task and transfers the picture you have just created into the storage area of your brain known as short-term memory.

But the picture does not die there. Your animal sees these pictures you send out, and picks up not only all the pictures, but also the feelings, emotions and ideas that accompany the picture as they go out telepathically from your mind through your physical body. You are constantly creating such pictures each time you think of something, and transmitting thoughts and emotions as you react to various stimuli during the course of your day. Though animals do learn the rudiments of human speech from living with us and react reliably to certain key words, it is the telepathic pictures, thoughts and emotions you send out that your animals use to make sense of you and the human world.

All animals speak this universal language, even species such as birds, turtles and fish. When I hear an 'expert' declaring certain animals to be dumb, it makes me sad, because I know from first-hand conversations with many different species how intelligent animals are. Often, as you will discover in this book, their stories are quite entertaining.

Not enough has been written about animal sensitivity, their intuition and intelligence, and the love and care they show to each other and to their humans. Pets are so like humans in their feelings and emotions, which makes them very sensitive to human emotions. They understand all the problems within their home. If the owner is depressed, they feel the unhappiness. If the owner is happy, they feel the same way.

This is not to anthropomorphize animals, but rather to acknowledge finally that they do experience emotions not too dissimilar from our own. Animals are certainly well aware of their own feelings, and pet owners and people who work closely with animals are quick to tell you their animal companions display behaviour that is difficult not to interpret as emotional. We've all seen dogs smiling and heard cats sighing with contentment.

Yet, until recently, the world of feelings was considered exclusively a human province. Fortunately, that is changing. Even scientists are now beginning to accept that animals do experience emotion, though they may be loth to attach that particular word to their observations. In their wonderful book, *When Elephants Weep*, Jeffrey Masson and Susan McCarthy make a convincing argument for the rich and complex emotional lives they have observed among animals in the wild.

But animals experience far more than simple emotion, far more than we give them credit for. They have incredible memories. They never forget when they have been hurt, and they never forget a kindness. If there is a change in their behaviour, I have come to understand that there is always a good reason for that change and that the reason, which may seem inexplicable to their humans, makes perfect sense when viewed from the animal's perspective. In fact, upon investigation, I often find the problem originates with the owner, not the animal.

If we as pet owners and animal lovers are sensitive and observant, then we, too, can understand our pets and their behaviour in new and rewarding ways. It is not difficult to do, though each of you will achieve varying degrees of success depending upon your openness to telepathic communication, your persistence, the relationship you have with your animals to begin with, and the animal's willingness to communicate telepathically and proficiency in doing so.

At the end of this book, I will explain how you may achieve a higher level of communication with the animals in your care. But first, I will tell you a little about my background, and how I came to this work of animal communication. Then I will share some of the wonderful stories of pets and their owners who have been helped by St Francis and my angel guides — some healed of an illness, some restored to their rightful homes after being lost, others simply guided into more desirable behaviour. I hope these stories will offer you insight into what your pets are thinking.

Whether or not you believe I can truly 'talk' to animals is unimportant. What matters is that you treat your pets with the greatest love, kindness and courtesy possible. With patience, sensitivity, awareness, and the conscientious application of the principles I have sought to employ in my relationships with members of the animal kingdom, principles which are outlined in this book, it is possible for many animal lovers to establish telepathic communication with their pets. If the stories in this book open the way for you to enhance and develop further the loving relationships you enjoy with your pets, I will have achieved my purpose.

St Francis has asked me to help animals, and I pass that request along to you. All that our pets want is love and security. It is my wish that after you read this book, you will have some insight into the importance of demonstrating that love to your pet on a daily basis.

CHAPTER I

Little pigs have big ears: my early life

When I was a child in England, I spent many happy hours talking to the animals in my village. It was not the imaginary talk so many children use; I actually communicated with animals and held daily conversations and consultations with my favourites. I found out their likes and dislikes, how they felt about each other, and what made them sad and happy.

In the typically egocentric way of a child, I thought everyone could talk to animals just like I did. I had no idea as yet that I was different in that respect, and that to other people the notion of actually communicating with animals in an intelligible way was completely unthinkable. So when I told my family I talked to animals, they thought I was simply being imaginative.

I lived with my parents, Russell and Cora Smith, my sisters Dawn and Coral and my brother Gordon in Hartwell, Northamptonshire. My father was a businessman in the village. He had a grocery and several other business concerns. There, I was known as 'Sunny' because of my outgoing disposition and golden blonde hair.

I was the third child, and spent a great deal of time with my maternal grandmother, Emmaline Robishaw, as my mother was busy working, and had little appreciation of what she called my 'vivid imagination'. I used to try to impress my mother by saying, 'I've been on my best behaviour, Mummy,' to which she'd reply, 'You haven't got any best behaviour, Sunny.'

My grandmother Robishaw was a very beautiful woman and I adored her. Her cottage was immaculately kept and provided me with a cosy retreat from the rigours of life with my family. We often sat together on the long winter evenings, while she taught me to sew, knit and read, hobbies which I enjoy to this day. I loved to operate her old treadle machine. I used my feet to push the platform back and forth, leaving my hands free to guide the fabric through the needle.

I had my own bedroom at my grandmother's cottage and lived mostly there rather than with my family. Grandmother's cottage was very close to my parents' home, so it was easy for me to go back and forth.

Grandmother gave me my own little corner of her cottage garden so I could grow flowers from seeds. She taught me how to put the seeds in the ground just so; then each day I would go with my little watering can and gently water them. My favourite time was when my hard work was rewarded with a garden full of fragrant, lovely blossoms.

Grandmother's cottage garden was spectacular, full of old-fashioned roses, lilacs and lots of other beautiful flowers. We spent many happy hours in her garden. That is where I first encountered frogs. Grandmother taught me how essential frogs were to the life of a garden because they ate all the insects.

She also taught me how clever the bees were. She used to say to me, 'See how the bees kiss the flowers?' She told me they did that to get the nectar which they then took back to their hive to make honey. I marvelled at how hard the bees worked to make honey, which I loved to eat.

Watching bees was just one of our pastimes. Grandmother taught me that I must always honour all creatures, no matter how insignificant they might seem to me. She said each one had its place in God's universe, and that if I was observant, I could begin to understand what that place was and how all animals worked together for the good of nature.

On summer evenings, the two of us would go for walks through Salcey Forest. When we happened upon a particularly beautiful spot, we put down a blanket and sat very quietly, not moving or making a sound. Those times were very special to me. We saw many beautiful forest creatures as we sat there: a shy and gentle family of deer, rabbits hopping across the clearing, red squirrels and bushy-tailed foxes. She understood that I could talk to animals in a way no other child of the village could and she made sure I had the opportunity to observe wild creatures in their natural habitats. Those times in Salcey Forest were wonderful for us both, and when I look back and remember today, it still brings me a feeling of happiness.

Back then I had a small terrier named Judy, my first dog. She would always tell me if she felt cold. Country winters can be bitter, and we often had snow. Animals do feel the cold, especially when there are drastic changes in temperature. When I told my parents that Judy was cold, Father said she had a fur coat to keep her warm enough. But I knew my father was wrong about that, as Judy transmitted her body temperature to me and I felt cold in my own body.

When Judy was cold, I would get one of my baby sister Coral's woollen knitted jackets and put it on her. Then I would lay her on the sofa and cover her with a blanket. She lay on her back with her little paws over the top of the blanket, telling me she felt very happy when she was warm, and very unhappy when she was cold.

I knew the blue and white striped jacket was Judy's favourite coat because she telepathically transmitted a picture of it to me. My family was amazed that the dog allowed me to do the things I did for her, because she could and did nip if someone tried to do something she did not like. But Judy always had a wonderful temperament around me, and we loved each other dearly. The difference with me was that I spoke to her telepathically, so I knew her likes and dislikes. I often told my mother that if people would listen to Judy, they would know what she wanted.

Some people are very active and talk with their hands, but Judy did not like people running about or moving their arms very quickly. It startled her and made her feel uncomfortable, so she nipped to let people know she did not like it. Nor did she like bicycles going very fast. She said it made her feel dizzy, so she chased them. I was careful always to move very slowly when I was with Judy so as not to alarm her.

Judy was approaching the end of her life, and I told her death was nothing to fear. I told Judy that when she died, she was going to heaven where God lived. My grandmother had told me God had a beautiful garden and lots of fields for the animals to play in. I told Judy that one day I would meet up with her and play with her in God's heavenly fields, and she would never be cold again.

As Judy grew older, I realized I could feel in my own body the aches and pains the old dog was experiencing. I learned how to soothe those aches by laying my small hands upon her body. I didn't truly understand what I was doing; I just knew I could do it. I also began to understand why she was often grumpy and cross with people. I envied her the option she had of simply nipping at people who annoyed her; it was something I frequently wished I could do. But I acted out my frustrations over my parents' indifference in the time-honoured fashion of any child who feels she has been neglected or misunderstood.

I did outrageous things, like putting our chickens over the fence into the neighbour's garden. Mr Breyfield was always complaining about my cats going into his garden, but that was nothing compared to the damage our chickens could do. I told the incredulous birds they could eat all Mr Breyfield's green vegetables and my all-too-willing accomplices didn't stop until their tummies were ready to burst. I was never found out. When asked, I told my father the gate between our two gardens must have been left open by accident. This was just one of my many adventures with my animal friends.

I soon became aware I could tune in to how any animal was feeling simply by concentrating. This being the 1940s, the baker, Mr Sturgess, went through the village with a horse-drawn cart delivering fresh bread. People would come out of their houses and shops to get a loaf and exchange a bit of gossip. When the baker's horse, Pickles, stopped outside my father's shop, I closed my eyes and my leg started aching. That's how I knew the old workhorse's leg was hurting, too. Soon, I realized Pickles was telling me about his sore leg, and asking for my help to feel better.

When I ran my hands gently over Pickles's face and asked him if he would allow me to help him with his pain, he always said yes. Because I was not yet tall enough to reach up to him, Pickles lowered his head for me so I could stroke him. I put my hands on his poor leg and stroked it, all the while telling him it would be better. I had a sensation of heat in my hands while I was doing this, and felt what I now know was healing energy flowing through me to the horse. Finally, the baker climbed back into his wagon, but not before the old horse thanked me for removing the soreness from his leg. Even the baker seemed to understand that I had a beneficial effect on Pickles, who could then complete his rounds in comfort, free from the pain and stiffness in his arthritic foreleg. That was when I discovered my gift for healing animals.

I loved the great old workhorse. Sometimes, Pickles asked me to go with them to complete their rounds. He said I could ride on his back. So I would ask Mr Sturgess to lift me up and I rode the rest of the way perched high upon my noble steed, feeling like a princess.

I liked to visit the old horse in his field when he wasn't at work pulling the baker's cart. I brought him apples and carrots, and we passed many a pleasant hour chatting amicably. Pickles grumbled because he had worked hard all his life, and did not want to go on working indefinitely. But he feared Mr Sturgess could not manage without him.

Though Mr Sturgess was a kindly man who treated Pickles with affection and respect, he was greatly dependent on the old horse. Pickles knew the baker's route by heart. He knew where Mr Sturgess had to go into a home to take bread to an invalid, and where people would come out to chat. Mr Sturgess feared he could never find another horse as well suited to the work as Pickles.

After the baker's round was completed, Mr Sturgess drove to the pub, where, like most men of the village, he enjoyed spending a couple of hours each day discussing news and downing a few pints of ale. Pickles dropped him off at the Rose and Crown, then pulled the empty wagon back home by himself. Once there, he pawed the ground outside the cottage door until Mrs Sturgess came to unharness him from the baker's cart and release him into the field. He did this every day except Sunday, which was his day off.

Mrs Sturgess really loved Pickles, and he loved her in return. She also treated the old horse with great kindness and love, stroking him as she unfastened his harness. She knew Pickles had arthritis, so she soothed him by telling him she had a lot of pain in her bones, too. 'I know your poor old bones hurt like mine, duck,' she told him affectionately.

Pickles was something of a sensation in our village. We all considered him a very clever horse for figuring out how to get himself home, and not waiting outside the pub in all sorts of weather for Mr Sturgess to finish his pint. When Mr Sturgess pulled up outside the Rose and Crown and tied the reins over the horse's head so that he would not catch them in his legs as he walked home, Pickles knew he had finished work for the day. 'Pickles, go and have your rest,' Mr Sturgess would say. We all knew the baker would stagger home a couple of hours later after having a few pints of beer.

Sometimes I was in the village and Pickles asked me to walk back home with him, which I always did. When the apple trees were heavy with fruit in the autumn, he liked to walk past Miss Bilton's, the schoolteacher's house, and help himself to a couple of choice apples. She didn't mind sharing as we were all fond of the horse. When he couldn't get over to Miss Bilton's, he often asked me to bring him apples in the field. Many times in the middle of a school day, Pickles telepathically sent me a picture of a rosy apple, and I knew he wanted me to bring him one after school. He liked ripe apples much more than green ones.

Pickles was great friends with Blackey, a lovely black pony who belonged to Derek, my brother Gordon's friend. Like Pickles, Blackey was also a working horse. He delivered milk from Derek's dairy farm to the lorry, which then took it to the factory where it was bottled.

Folly Farm was about three miles from the village. At about the age of 24, Derek had taken it over after the death of his father. I spent many an idyllic afternoon ambling along the road to the dairy, picking poppies, buttercups and daisies, and talking with my animal friends along the way. I knew all the cows by name as English farmers in those days had the habit of naming each of their milk cows. I made up names for the sheep and called out to them as they grazed in the lush fields and pastures adjoining the road. Sometimes, so many cows and sheep followed me along the road and through the fields that it looked as if I was leading a herd.

Derek's wife, Hill (short for Hilda), did most of the actual physical labour on the farm. She milked the dairy herd twice a day while her husband went fishing. The cows all walked up to the top of the hill when it was milking time. When the milking was done, Hill loaded the milk cans into the cart, and Blackey pulled the cart up to the factory. After his work was done, Hill turned Blackey out into the field to graze and relax a bit. On some days when I asked for a ride, Blackey said yes. But on other days, he said no and no matter how I tried to convince him, he wouldn't be caught. He'd run full speed in the opposite direction, tossing his shiny black mane and tail as if to say, 'Not today! You can't have a ride today!' But on those days when he did allow me to ride, Blackey took great care of me. He would not buck or run too fast.

When we rambled along the country lanes together, Blackey often stopped to nibble on grass. I liked to get off his back and point out particularly succulent patches, calling out, 'Look, Blackey! There's some juicy grass over there!' Then I would sit at his feet while he ate.

Sometimes I harnessed Blackey to his trap and went to my father's shop in the village to fetch groceries for Hill. I always made sure to get a big, juicy apple for Blackey.

Blackey enjoyed visiting Pickles as much as I did. The two were great friends. I used to tell them how important they were because they worked so hard and were so vital to the commerce of the village.

There was another horse in the field next to Pickles, a beautiful horse named Star. All she had to do was take Mr Smart's daughter Sue for the occasional ride. Both Blackey and Pickles thought Star was cosseted and spoiled, but they liked her nonetheless and admired her great beauty.

All three horses were frightened of the village blacksmith, whom they said was not very kind to them. Blackey and Pickles told me they had heard him saying that horses were stupid, and that I was stupid as well for all the fantastic stories I made up about being able to talk to animals.

Blackey and Pickles told me what happened to old Mrs Bobbitt's horse, Rosy, after she died. Mrs Bobbitt had placed the animal in the blacksmith's care, and asked him to make sure her beloved horse went to a good home. Instead, he had sold Rosy to the slaughterhouse for meat. Blackey and Pickles begged me to convince their respective owners not to leave them in the blacksmith's care should they pass on, and so I did.

The blacksmith regularly went into my father's store to buy a meat pie for his noon meal. One day he came in and ordered his usual and I called out, 'Let me get it for you, Dad.' My father was more than happy to let me assist him, as he liked to exchange news and gossip with his customers, and the blacksmith was no exception.

I never could understand how the blacksmith could criticize other people when he himself was the talk of the village, always visiting Mrs Biggles whenever her husband was away from home. I often overheard people telling my father, 'There he is at Mrs Biggles's again, and she with her curtains drawn for hours. I think it's disgusting!' When I asked my dad what was disgusting about Mrs Biggles and the blacksmith, he just replied, 'Little pigs have big ears!'

On this particular day I decided to punish the blacksmith for his unkindness to Pickles and Blackey, and for what he did to Rosy. Before I gave him his pie, I smothered it in a cloud of black pepper, then wrapped it in grease-proof paper and handed it to him with a big smile. Then I slipped off to the back room where I could watch as he took his first bite. The blacksmith started to choke and his face turned bright red. At that point I made a hasty exit via the back door of my father's shop and hid myself away for a while, at least until I stopped laughing.

When I arrived back home in time for tea, Father said he wanted to see me. He asked me if I had put pepper in the blacksmith's meat pie. He had found the pepper pot in the shop almost empty and the day before it had been almost full. I told him no, that it must have been an accident at the factory. My father was very angry and told me I had to stack shelves in the store for the next week. I hated stacking shelves but it was worth the punishment just to see the satisfaction on the faces of Pickles and Blackey when I told them the story. I decided that from then on, if I could find any way to annoy the blacksmith, I would.

*

The annual village fete was a big occasion. One year, I asked Pickles if I could ride him in the parade. He liked that idea very much. I communicated to Pickles that I was going to wear a pretty dress, and that he would have a ribbon in his harness. He immediately transmitted that he wanted a red ribbon, so I told him red it would be.

When the big day arrived, I got up early. Mr Sturgess had told me I would have to give Pickles a bath before the parade and brush his coat until it shone. Pickles was excited about the parade and felt very happy that I was going to be riding him. I told him he was a special horse because not many horses got to walk in the fete parade; in fact, this particular year he was the only one.

I brushed his mane and plaited his tail, telling him all the while how smart he looked. Pickles said he hadn't had his tail plaited before, so I reminded him of the week before when I had shown him my own hair done up in a plait, and told him he would be having his tail done the same way. That pleased him immensely.

As Pickles did not have a saddle, I rode directly on his back. The old horse was used to walking with his head down to bear the weight of the baker's cart. But I trans-mitted a feeling to him of standing straight and tall. I told him that today he would walk with his head held high and proud, because he was my special horse.

As I rode Pickles up the road, he told me he would walk his very best and that he hoped that bad dog, Hero, who always chased him and tried to nip his legs, would not be at the parade. I told him not to worry, that nothing could spoil this day for us. I told him we were going to win the competition and when we did, I would get him a lot of apples as a reward. I told him we would get a ribbon and a present if we won a prize. He was even more excited about the prospect than I was.

We did get third prize and I told Pickles that I would remember the day as long as I lived. I told him I could not have won if it had not been for him, and promised to bring him apples in the field every day. Whenever we spoke of this occasion, he transmitted feelings of joy, love and pride.

Looking back, one of my fondest memories is of the old horse pulling his cart through the village, with his tattered third-prize ribbon still hanging from his harness, where he insisted it should stay.

Other animals often joined Pickles in our conversations. We discussed the weather, and I remember clearly how the cows complained about the rain, how they hated the misery they endured as the cold drizzle fell on them. They had no shelter, no place to get away from the weather. They told me their favourite time was when the sun was shining. Then you would pass the field and see them looking content, their faces inclined towards the warm rays.

My favourite topic for discussion with my animal friends was the village news or, to put it more plainly, gossip. Some animals, the more curious ones, knew everything about everyone and were eager to tell all. They accepted the foibles of their human companions and were not judgmental, but often they had a hard time understanding the complexities of human behaviour. They especially didn't understand Tappy, who was unkind to his wife and children. The cat at the confectionery told us that no matter how many times he had beaten her during the week, Tappy always bought his wife a big box of chocolates when he got paid, to make up for his rages. The cat thought it a poor exchange for a life of terror, and we all agreed.

Following these gossip sessions, I often got into trouble with my mother for knowing something I wasn't supposed to know. If I had been wise, I would have said nothing, but I was just as eager to share the village gossip with my family as the animals were to share it with me. Mother could never track down the source of my knowledge. When she asked me how I knew so much, and I told her such and such a dog or cat had told me, she just got angrier. 'Little pigs have big ears,' she would say, just like my dad, not realizing how true her statement was.

One day my father came home with three goose eggs and told my mother they were for me. He told me if I put them under a chicken and kept an eye on them, the eggs would hatch out. I was very happy to think I would have my own geese.

The chicken sat on the goose eggs for a number of weeks, and I made daily inspections to see if any little goslings had pecked their way out. One day I was thrilled to find one already halfway out of its shell. Then two days later the other two geese followed.

I finally felt I had my own little family. The three goslings, responding to my love and kindness, followed me everywhere. I named them after my favourite flowers of the field: Buttercup, Daisy and Primrose. As they got older, they began to communicate with me like all the other animals. We would sit and chat for hours in the field near the hen house.

On Saturdays, I dressed up and went with my grandmother on the bus to nearby Northampton to help her with the shopping. I cherished these times alone with my grandmother and tried to be on my best behaviour. Still, my geese walked with me to the bus stop, and waited with me until the bus came, at which point I told them to go home. My new dog, Silky, a Golden Retriever, accompanied the geese. When the bus pulled away, he saw them safely home.

My geese and Silky even went with me to school each day, going as far as the school gate and waiting until the whistle blew. When class started, my animals went back to the field by the hen house. At break time they returned to share a bit of cheese sandwich with me. After break, they returned home once again and when the school day was over, I joined them there.

Some of the other children were amazed at my entourage. They thought it was strange having geese as pets, but I didn't care. With my geese, I had security and a sense that they belonged to me.

One day, the geese told me they had something special to share. Primrose, who was always in charge by virtue of being the largest and most determined of the three, marched forward, breathless with the news that Silky was going to have puppies. She had overheard my father telling Mr Webster that news. No sooner had she relayed the information than Buttercup asked me, 'What are puppies?' I explained, within the confines of my limited understanding, that puppies were baby dogs put into Silky's tummy one night by a fairy.

'How do they get out?' Buttercup asked.

'When they are ready, they just pop out,' I replied. Then all three geese declared they would like to have some puppies, too.

I explained further that geese didn't have puppies; they had baby geese, which came out in the form of eggs. This didn't sound nearly as intriguing as having puppies in their tummies, so they all decided to give up the idea of reproducing themselves. Instead, they declared, they would help Silky with her puppies when the time came.

Each evening, my geese went with me while I shut the hens up in the hen house. I told them they had to stay in their little goose house at night for protection from the foxes. I told them foxes did bad things to geese and hens, so they listened and stayed inside their little house all night long until I came back and let them out the next morning.

This happy relationship continued for almost nine months. I spent idyllic days in the company of my beloved animals, chattering away with them about many interesting subjects. I told them everything – how I did in school, what were my favourite and least favourite subjects – and they listened as if I were the most fascinating child in the world. They commiserated with me about my family problems, and I listened to all their intrigues.

There was a dog in the village named Hero whom none

of them could stand as he had a bad temper. They often regaled me with tales of their latest encounter with that dreadful dog, but compassionately acknowledged that Hero couldn't help himself because he had a mean human for an owner.

My animals explained to me that most humans did not take the time to talk with them as I did. Most humans, they said, could not understand them when they spoke. Though I'd had inklings of this, this was the first confirmation that my ability to communicate telepathically with animals was unusual.

My geese liked being in the field with their namesakes, the buttercups and daisies. I even made daisy chains and put one round the neck of each goose and my dog too. I made one for myself as well, and people would smile at me with my menagerie of pets, all of us bedecked with daisies.

I remember how pleased the geese were that they didn't have to go to school. They wondered why I had to go. I told them that's just what human children did, that I had to go to school to learn. 'Learn what?' they queried. 'You already know everything important.' They couldn't conceive of making a child sit indoors all day, away from the fields and the flowers and animals of nature. They told me they missed my company while I was in school, and longed for the hour of my return.

I remember this period as a golden time, in which I was surrounded by the love of my animals and my grandmother Robishaw. With her I had a feeling of belonging, a feeling I didn't have with the rest of my family. I often asked my mother if I had been adopted, because I felt so different from the others. But my grandmother understood me, understood the incredible gift of animal communication I had been given, because she herself was clairvoyant and often had premonitions.

My grandmother also helped me learn how to communicate better with humans despite my hearing loss. As a young woman, she had worked in the cotton mills of Lancashire. Normal speech was impossible because of the noise from the machinery, so the young girls who worked there learned to read each other's lips. It was this skill that Emmaline taught me, and it helped me feel more connected to the human world.

I began to realize that not all people loved animals as I did, or harboured the same tender feelings. I wondered why so many adults believed they were superior to animals. To me, human behaviour was far worse and more unpredictable than animal behaviour, and I liked the animals much more than some humans (and still do).

Animals always had perfectly reasonable explanations for everything they did, and never deliberately hurt one another as the humans of my acquaintance often did. I began to realize that my ability to communicate with animals was something that no one could understand, much less believe in, except for my grandmother. Finally, my family's impatience with my 'imaginativeness' began to make sense. They truly did not believe I could talk to animals. Such a thing was outside their experience.

Then came the Christmas of 1950. I had been out riding with friends at a nearby farm. It was a Sunday, and Sunday lunch was always a big event — roast meat, vegetables and stuffing, and rice pudding or apple pie with custard for dessert. This particular occasion was made even grander because it was Christmas week, so my mother had decided to prepare a special meal.

I changed for lunch, being careful to wash my hands and brush my hair before presenting myself at the table. When I sat down, my mother came in carrying a steaming platter, smiling broadly as my father announced, 'We've got goose today!' Mother put the platter down on the table in front of my father so he could carve the bird, and then I realized I was looking at one of my beloved friends who had been killed and served up as a special treat.

I was stunned. I couldn't cry or even speak, I was so choked with emotion. Then I felt tears running down my face and I started sobbing. I felt my heart had been torn in two parts. I got up and ran away from the table, out to the garden where my geese always were. None of them was there. I ran to the goose house, but they were not there, either. I looked frantically from place to place, visiting all their favourite haunts, searching desperately for the other two geese.

Finally, I went into the barn. There in full view were my beautiful friends – dead, hanging by their feet from the rafters, blood dripping from their mouths. My father had killed all three geese, planning to give the other two as Christmas gifts to families in the village.

Raising stock for food was a way of life in the English village, particularly just after the war when meat was in scarce supply and rationing was still in force. What my father had done was routine for him and for the other members of my family. For me, it was a horror. I felt all the pain and terror the geese had felt. I sat and looked at their dead, cold bodies and sobbed and sobbed. A part of me had died with my beloved friends. The innocent happiness of my childhood had been cruelly torn away.

At that moment, overwhelmed with anguish and pain and knowing I could not allow myself to feel this heartbreak ever again, I forced a door in my mind shut for what I thought would be for ever. Though I still loved my animals and doted upon them, I would not allow myself to communicate with them in that special way, so that I could understand their thoughts, feelings and desires, and tell them my own in return. It was to protect myself from the anguish of my little family's horrible deaths that I vowed I would never again open myself up to an animal's pain and suffering.

My grandmother helped me perfect my lip-reading skills so I could function more easily in the human world, and as I matured, I left the world of animal communication behind. For the next forty years, my determination to forget held firm.

CHAPTER 2

Animals tell the best gossip: the beginning of my animal communication

It was the spring of 1994, and I was tired. I was in my studio in the Galleria area of Houston, where I and my daughter Emma had settled in order to start a business teaching American and European etiquette. The business was going well, but I was putting in long hours to build it up.

One day, after a particularly busy morning, I went to sit for a moment on the sofa in my studio and relax with a cup of coffee. Suddenly, I thought I saw something out of the corner of my eye, so I turned to look. Above one of the large mirrors on the wall, I saw a bright white light building up in the room. I realized it was the top half of an angel with large wings. She had a beautiful and gentle face. I knew the angel was going to speak to me.

'You will be doing God's work,' the angel said. 'You will be working with and for animals,' the angel continued, then she left.

I sat quietly, wondering what sort of work it would be. I was speechless, overwhelmed. I wondered what had just happened. I didn't know it yet, but in a matter of weeks, the channel of energy flowing between me and the animal kingdom would become so powerful it would completely override my childhood vow to shut out the voices of my animal friends.

For two weeks, nothing more transpired. I stayed so busy with my etiquette business I had little time to think about the angel's visit or what it meant. At home one morning, I went into my dressing room to put on my make-up and became aware of a presence behind me. I asked the visitor, 'Who are you?' And he answered, 'I am St Francis, the patron saint of animals. I am going to be working with you to help and heal animals.'

That was all the saint said. I sat down to ponder what the visitations meant. I was beginning to have faint recollections from my childhood, faded memories struggling back to life within some forgotten corner of my mind. Something was nibbling at the edges of my consciousness — thoughts, feelings I couldn't quite get hold of. The door was opening a little further, but it would still be weeks before I completely grasped the significance of my two heavenly visitations and began to understand what I know now, the course of my true life's work.

In common with many English people of my generation, I was raised as what you might call 'non-practising C of E'. It was certainly not a strongly Christian upbringing, churchgoing confined mostly to christenings, marriages and funerals, interspersed with the odd Christmas service. In adult life I came not to embrace any particular creed, and in fact have an acute distaste for the problems I see organized religion having caused for the lives of millions around the world.

However, I do consider myself a religious person, in the sense that I have convictions based on the belief that a deity or God-force exists within all of us. I believe in the sanctity of life in what might be termed a Buddhist sense, but I am not judgmental and believe that everybody has the right to determine their own set of religious, moral and ethical convictions, and live their lives accordingly. Nonetheless, this encounter was quite outside the bounds of what you might call my 'normal' spiritual sensibilities.

For a while, I was still a bit puzzled. I tried to understand what St Francis had meant when he told me he was going to be working with me to help and heal animals. I remembered an incident that had happened in England before I moved to America. Late one evening, my husband Fitz had come in and made a big fuss over our cat, Wellington, who is quite an elegant and sophisticated animal. As Wellington tried to leave the room a few minutes later, Bella, our beloved Rhodesian Ridgeback, bit him, drawing blood from the cat's neck. The attack amazed me because the animals had lived together in perfect harmony for years.

When I went to America, Fitz moved into the guest apartment on the top floor of the main house in Aston le Walls. Wellington preferred to remain in the main house, which he liked to patrol, while Bella moved to the guest apartment with Fitz. The tenants who rented the main house loved cats and doted upon Wellington. But the attack bothered me, and it worried me to leave my pets behind.

After the first year, the tenants left and Fitz moved back into the big house, putting the two animals back together again. Over in America, I started to worry when I heard this news, concerned that Bella's obvious jealousy might mean trouble for Wellington. I asked Fitz to be especially watchful once the two animals were reunited, to ensure that Bella did not repeat her attack.

I expressed my fears to a number of friends, and one friend recommended a respected animal communicator known as Florance who lived in California. I phoned and told Florance my story. She promised she would try to contact the animals the next morning after returning from church. But she was concerned about the distance involved as she had never tried to communicate with an animal so far away. I reminded her that telepathic communication knew no limits of time or distance, and was surprised to discover she did not know this. Florance told me that when she was ready to communicate, she just relaxed and it came to her. At that point, I wasn't even sure how I knew it, but I understood intuitively that I was right about time and distance being no object. I spoke with conviction of this belief and Florance agreed to try to get in touch with my animals to discover the problem.

The next day I rang the communicator again and discovered that she had, in fact, been able to contact my pets in England. To my astonishment, we found Bella blamed herself for my departure to America, assuming I had left home because I was angry about the attack on Wellington. According to the communicator, Bella was very upset about my absence, and wanted to know when I would return to England. Wellington told Florance he wasn't bothered about Bella's jealousy; he just stayed out of her way. But he did miss me and also wanted to know when I would return.

I realized the information the woman had given me was absolutely accurate, completely typical of my two pets' disparate personalities. The incident turned a key in my mind and made me waken to some forgotten memory; I knew I could do this sort of work also.

I decided to test my own powers of animal communication. I remembered I had once been able to do this with ease, and suspected this gift was what St Francis had been referring to when he told me I would be helping animals.

Each day at the same time, I started to speak to my animals. I visualized my home in England, and tried to speak to Bella and Wellington. I kept the conversation up for two weeks without receiving anything back, but I went on trying. I had promised myself I would continue for three months to see if the experiment would work.

One evening, I was booked as the speaker at a social gathering for a businesswomen's club in Houston. Just before dinner was served, I suddenly heard my dog Bella speaking to me telepathically.

'Why haven't you answered me?' Bella demanded. 'I've been talking and talking to you and you haven't answered. Are you still angry with me because I bit Wellington?'

I practically jumped from my chair. I told my daughter, Emma, who knew I had been trying to establish contact with my pets, that Bella had suddenly come through and was talking to me and sending me pictures. It was my first realization that animals communicate primarily by transmitting pictures of what they are talking about.

'When are you coming home?' Bella wanted to know. 'We all miss you. Everybody here is sad without you.'

I was overjoyed to hear my dog's voice. Suddenly Wellington chimed in with all the gossip of my village back home. In his wanderings about Aston le Walls, the inquisitive cat had picked up the local titbits. He told me that

Daisy, an elderly woman in the village, had gone into hospital, a fact which I verified in my next telephone conversation with Fitz. Bella then complained that the cleaning lady didn't clean the house the same way that 'Mummy' cleaned it and I laughed. Bella also said Fitz was annoyed because the car had broken down, and that she was sad because my mother, who had been to stay for a few weeks, had returned to her own home and Bella missed her.

All this was going on in a roomful of women who were expecting, within a matter of minutes, a speech on the finer points of etiquette. I could not get over my amazement. Somehow I had known that I could do it, that I had the gift of communicating with animals through mind energy, but I couldn't explain how I knew this. I gathered myself and stood up to walk to the podium. I tried to organize my thoughts for my speech while Bella and Wellington's voices were still ringing in my mind. I thought briefly that if I told my audience of my incredible experience, some would think I was stark raving mad.

I delivered my speech, but I couldn't wait to get into the car with Emma, to discuss what had happened with Bella and Wellington.

From that time on, I talked to my animals every day. Wellington continued in his role of village gossip, while Bella tried to determine when I would be coming home. I asked them to love and take care of each other, and Fitz reported a change in the relationship of the former rivals. Then one day, Bella reported being cross with Wellington because he had killed a bird and put it under a table in the house. Bella told the mighty hunter off, reminding him that

I didn't like it either when he stalked birds. Fitz reported that Bella barked and barked at Wellington the day he killed the bird. I was daily becoming more convinced of the accuracy of my communication with my animals. Everything they told me Fitz confirmed, and I had no other possible way to get the information that Bella and Wellington transmitted during their daily conversations.

When Fitz relayed the story of Bella's anger with Wellington, suddenly the reason for the previous attack became clear to me. Each year, the swallows returned from Africa to nest in the old barns, stables and outbuildings on our property. It was an event that filled us with joy, not only because of the beauty of the birds, but because their return signalled the end of the long, cold English winter, and the promise of warm, sunny spring days ahead.

We looked forward to the return of the swallows each spring, and to the birth of their babies as they nested on our land. We sat in our beautiful cottage garden each evening, surrounded by fragrant lupins, hollyhocks, honeysuckle and tree roses, enjoying a glass of wine and the soaring flight of the swallows. I knew that many of the swallows perished along the way, so I felt a special responsibility to care for the survivors who showed up faithfully in my garden each spring.

When the baby swallows were learning to fly, many of them dropped into the grass, a perfect opportunity for a marauding cat. I always tried to keep Wellington in the house during the few days the babies were testing their wings. But Wellington, like all cats, would manage to find a way out. His hunting instinct was deeply ingrained.

One day Wellington killed two baby swallows and that

upset me very much. Bella heard me scolding him and became angry because she knew Wellington had done something to anger me. Unbeknown to us, she decided to try to help with this problem. She took it upon herself to punish Wellington for his transgressions and that was the reason she went for him, not jealousy as I had supposed. Of course, I had no way of knowing Bella's line of reasoning at the time, because I had not yet re-established my ability to communicate with animals telepathically.

As my confidence in my ability to communicate with animals grew, I began to share with a few close friends the details of the remarkable thing that had happened to me. When I first started my animal communication business, not many of my friends knew exactly what I was doing. They thought of me as a British etiquette expert, and there was not always a convenient time or place to tell them how my life was changing as I was led more and more towards working full time with animals.

Then Stacey, my friend who had recommended the animal communicator in California, asked me to talk to her two cats, Hubert and Leonard, to see if I could help with a couple of behavioural problems that had developed. I agreed, feeling ready to tackle whatever assignment St Francis might send my way. I knew I had embarked on my true life's mission.

CHAPTER 3

No bad pets: fighting and other behaviour problems

Perhaps no problem is more distressing to pet owners than when a beloved and normally well-behaved pet starts acting up in ways that are unusual. Just as upsetting is when once peaceful housemates begin fighting. Many of my clients consult me about this type of problem, and they are usually so distraught it has brought them to the brink of giving up the animal for adoption or, in the case of an animal that is biting or attacking, having it put to sleep. Of course, no animal lover wants to do that.

Like all problems with animals, undesirable behaviour can be resolved by employing a bit of keen observation to try to determine what has upset your pet. Remember, animals are like children in that they crave our attention and affection. When they feel they are being ignored, they find ways to get the attention they desire, and they really don't care whether it is positive or negative attention. All they know is that if they misbehave, their owner who has been overlooking them will sit up and take notice of the pet. The worse the lack of attention is, the worse you can expect your pet's behaviour to become.

You can tell many things about your pet's mood just by

observing its body language, which is easy to read and requires no special training to interpret. If your pet's ears are down, or it goes down on its tummy and has a forlorn look about its face, you can be sure something is upsetting it.

You do not have to have any special gifts to observe your pet, just the ability to think about the circumstances which led up to the start of the behaviour problem. When you identify an element that has changed, more than likely you will have discovered the cause of the misbehaviour.

Animals are concerned about any change in their household. Often pet owners make important decisions without considering how they will affect their pets. Remember that pets are very sensitive to the human emotions swirling around them. It is important to tell your pets the truth about any changes in the household. Help them to understand the situation, particularly if the change is to be permanent, as in the case of a divorce or a death in the family.

Even when the change is not necessarily permanent, as when a child leaves for college, it is important to let your pet know what is happening. If you fail to explain to a pet why a change is taking place, the animal has a tendency to blame itself for the problem, as in the case of my Bella, who thought her attack on Wellington was what caused me to leave home for America.

Hubert

My friend Stacey, who is normally sensitive to her pets'
needs, called me with a problem she was having with her
cat Hubert. Hubert is one of a pair of grey tabby brothers,
and is somewhat temperamental and highly strung, while
his brother Leonard is more laid back. The two cats were
used to sleeping with Stacey every night. This arrangement
was mutually satisfactory for both human and cats.

Suddenly, Hubert started waking Stacey around 3 a.m.
by jumping on her chest. If that didn't have the desired
effect, he would go to the mini blinds over the dresser and
rattle them with his paws, almost as if he was playing a
xylophone, until Stacey had no choice but to get up from
the bed to stop him. She was becoming angrier with each
passing night, and getting cross from lack of sleep.

In desperation, she called me and asked for help. At that
point, I was still experimenting with communicating with
my own animals, Bella and Wellington. But I agreed to
do my best.

I was surprised at how easily I connected telepathically
with the cats. I asked Hubert why he was being so naughty
and waking up his mummy every night. He quickly told
me he was angry because Stacey hadn't been spending much
time at home lately. In fact, he said, Stacey hardly ever
spent any time with them any more, so he woke her up in
the middle of the night because then he was sure he would
have her full if angry attention, which he thought was better
than no attention at all.

Hubert seemed to realize he had an attentive audience,
so he continued to list his complaints. He was upset because

it had been a while since Stacey had served tuna fish, his favourite food. He wanted tuna more often, he told me, and couldn't understand why they didn't have it any more. He also was missing his little red ball, which had disappeared some time earlier, and he wanted a new ball to replace it. Finally, he complained that he had a new scratching post, and he liked his old one better.

I called Stacey and told her what Hubert had told me, and she admitted that her work had been greatly occupying her attention lately. She said she arrived home late, and then was so exhausted she hadn't been giving her two cats their accustomed playtime. She was also surprised to realize she had inadvertently dropped tuna from the cats' diet. She had run out and simply hadn't had a chance to go to the store where she bought her favourite brand. In fact she hadn't served it to the cats in almost three months.

She laughed when I told her about the red ball, and told me that Hubert kept it with him constantly. Quite tidy by nature, Stacey said she had thrown the ball out because it was looking so shabby, never realizing it would upset Hubert. She promised to pay more attention to the cats, and to go straight out and buy some tuna and a new red ball, and to bring back the old, favoured scratching post.

I then told Stacey she had to make sure she spent adequate time with her pets on a regular basis, or the problem would persist. I also told Hubert he mustn't wake Stacey up in the middle of the night. Hubert agreed to behave himself, but only if Stacey would spend more time with him during the evening hours. He also insisted that Stacey had to give him her entire attention. That interested me. He told me that even when Stacey spent time with him, often she was in the kitchen or the bathroom attending to other business. He transmitted a picture to me of the way he wanted Stacey to communicate with him, face to face.

Stacey started laughing when I described the transmission, admitting she often did talk to her pets from another room while she was cooking or washing or putting on her make-up. This partial attention didn't bother Leonard at all, who was quite certain of Stacey's love and unconcerned if she missed the occasional ear scratch. But Hubert, who has a more insecure nature, simply wasn't going to put up with this lack of attention a moment longer without letting Stacey know he was upset. I told Stacey atypical behaviour is one of the few ways that animals have to get their owner's attention when they don't like something that is going on.

Stacey made the requested changes, pulling Hubert into her lap for a cuddle each night. Tuna was reintroduced to the diet, and a new red ball obtained. Within a few days, Hubert's nocturnal rampages stopped and he resumed his former exemplary behaviour.

It is important to make sure that when you give time to your animal you offer quality attention. Make sure you go down to their level on the floor or bring them into your lap, establish eye contact and give them your whole attention, petting and talking to them. Remember that animals are very sensitive to materials. They like the feel of some fabrics more than others. If the fabric you are wearing is slippery or rough, your pet may not wish to lie down or sit in your lap. Cats love to knead cloth, particularly soft blankets and comforters.

Some people have a problem with cats scratching their furniture. Scratching is both natural and necessary for cats, to keep their claws healthy. I am completely opposed to the declawing of cats. It is inhumane and causes horrible pain, and often produces a cat which bites, as they have no other defence after their claws are removed. This is another example of an animal behaviour problem that is produced by a mistake on the part of the human.

Often scratching is a result of poor training (or no training) or the use of an inadequate scratching post. Scratching posts should be substantial, tall and wide enough to bear the weight of the cat without wobbling as he stretches his body and exercises his claws. It is important for the board to be big enough for a cat to hook its claws in the top while stretching his entire body and exercising all his muscles. Cats cannot scratch properly on a round, narrow scratching post. When that is all that is provided, cats will often prefer to scratch a sofa or chair, especially if they haven't been trained that scratching furniture is undesirable behaviour.

There is a simple, humane way to train cats away from furniture. Keep a spray mister of plain, room-temperature water handy, and whenever your cat scratches furniture, say 'No!' sharply, spray it with water and take it to its scratching board. The hissing sound of the sprayer and the feel of the water combine to give your cat a most unpleasant experience, at least in its estimation. Eventually, they will learn that the furniture is off-limits. But remember, this training will work properly only if you provide an adequate alternative scratching surface.

Pebbles

I had a call from my client, Luan, a lovely Chinese lady whose pets I had worked with many times. She was upset because Pebbles, one of her three cats, had suddenly forced Timmy, another of her cats, into a corner and wouldn't let him come out. Every time poor Timmy tried to leave the corner, Pebbles would attack him, biting and scratching, until Timmy had no choice but to retreat. The one time Luan tried to intervene, Pebbles had bitten her, too – a fact that amazed her, because in their seven years together the cat had never been anything other than a loving and gentle companion.

I connected to Pebbles telepathically. He was very angry. I asked him why he was upset and he sent me back a funny sensation in my nose, and a picture of Timmy. I asked Pebbles, 'Why are you attacking Timmy?'

Pebbles responded quite simply, 'Timmy has a strange scent. If he moves out of the corner he will make everywhere smell strange.'

The explanation for the uncomfortable feeling in my nose was clear, but I still didn't know why Pebbles had bitten Luan. 'Why did you bite Luan, Pebbles? You have never bitten before.'

'If she had picked Timmy up, she would have smelled like him, so I bit her to keep her from picking him up,' Pebbles said.

Seen from the point of view of the animal, it was all so logical. I asked Luan if she had put a new spray or powder on Timmy and she told me she'd bought a new homeopathic flea remedy because Timmy had a terrible infestation of fleas, and she was afraid to use a poison on him. I wondered when she had employed the new treatment and she told me a few days before. Then I asked her if this was when Pebbles had changed his behaviour towards Timmy, and she answered that it was. Pebbles, compared to most cats, has a heightened sense of smell. I reminded Luan of a previous incident with Pebbles when he had reacted to the scent of a new perfume she had started wearing by refusing to come near her. Apparently, the odour of the flea remedy was also offensive to his sensitive nose.

'It smells okay to me,' Luan said, 'and it has gotten rid of the fleas.'

'Well, it doesn't smell okay to Pebbles,' I told her. 'You didn't put this preparation on him?'

Luan said she had not because Pebbles did not have a flea problem.

I then explained that the awful smell was what had upset Pebbles and caused him to attack both her and Timmy. I advised her to bathe Timmy immediately with plain water and a gentle shampoo to get rid of the smell, and also to wash her hands thoroughly. I told her not to use this remedy again.

Luan called me a few days later to explain that once she bathed Timmy and got rid of the smell, things went back to normal in her house, with the two cats resuming their close, loving relationship.

While we are on the subject of fleas, I want to mention the chemical flea poisons which are so popular. While they certainly kill fleas on contact, they are also toxic to your dogs and cats, and also some people. There have been many cases where an application of a flea spray, powder or dip has produced tragic results. These deadly chemicals accumulate in your pets' bodies, and can affect their lungs, heart, intestines, skin, liver and kidneys. Many animals have died as a result of a toxic build-up of these chemicals in their bodies over a period of time.

Though Luan was certainly right to try a homeopathic remedy to combat her flea problem, Pebbles simply didn't appreciate the one she selected, so she will try others until she finds one that is suitable.

I use a simple trick to keep my house free of fleas without the use of poisons. Fleas are attracted to light, so I put a small light bulb above a bowl of soapy water in every room. When they try to jump up to the light, they land in the water and cannot escape.

You can also sprinkle plain borax powder on your carpet. The powder penetrates the fleas' hard bodies and literally dries them out, causing their death. Leave it in place twenty-four hours and then vacuum off. Keep your pets away from the carpet while the borax powder is in place, so that they don't pick it up on their paws and lick it. After you vacuum, the carpet will be safe for them again.

Amadeus

One day I received a call from Rhonda, whose dog, Amadeus, was training to be a member of the Houston Flyball Association. Amadeus was in danger of being dropped from the flyball team because of his aggressive behaviour towards the other dogs on the team.

When Amadeus arrived with Rhonda, he walked across

my studio looking and sniffing everywhere, then asked me where the other dogs were. I told him there were no other dogs here. He then asked where the cats were as he lived with nineteen cats. I said, 'There are no cats, just you.'

Amadeus had picked up the scents of the other animals who'd been to see me. Because he was so interested in investigating all the intriguing smells, it took him quite a while to settle down. When animals are taken from their familiar environments and brought to my office, they are excited or nervous, or sometimes even a bit upset. Since I can communicate telepathically with animals immediately through their owners' energy, I normally prefer that owners consult me without their animals present, to save the twenty or thirty minutes it usually takes for the pet to calm down and become receptive to telepathic communication. I'll make an exception when an animal is sick and needs hands-on healing. In this case, I didn't know until she got to my studio that Rhonda was bringing the dog with her. Once she arrived, there was no sense in making her leave.

Rhonda told me Amadeus refused to go into the box to pick up the flyball. I asked her to draw a chart of the actual run and tell me what duties were expected of the dog in the competition. Rhonda explained the course, but said that Amadeus attacked any other dog that came near him.

I asked Amadeus why he attacked the other dogs. He told me that at one time he had been a cattle dog on a ranch and he didn't like the cattle bumping him. He was afraid the other dogs were going to bump him if he let them get too near. I assured him the other dogs had no intention of bumping him as the cattle had so often done, and told him the other dogs meant him no harm; that they were simply trying to do well in the competition.

I asked him if he wanted to compete with the other dogs and he said yes, but was unsure about what he had to do. I told him he had to go into the box and pick up the ball with his mouth. When I transmitted this picture to him, Amadeus told me he finally understood what was wanted.

Then Rhonda told me he wasn't very good on the lead. I asked him why he wouldn't sit and why he wouldn't do what his owner requested when she pulled on the lead, a method of control commonly used during flyball competitions. Then his sad story came out. He told me that his former owner tied him up very tightly with thin string that cut into his neck, and it had hurt him badly. He had been pulled along with the string and tied to a tree with it. His neck had been rubbed raw. Although he knew Rhonda would never hurt him because she loved him very much, each time she pulled him a certain way it reminded him of the pain he had experienced in the past and this confused him.

I repeated the story to Rhonda, and she told me how Amadeus had been taken from his previous owner because he had been treated so badly. She had adopted him from the Humane Society, and she did not know much about his background, but now she understood why the problems had occurred. She asked me to tell Amadeus she would not pull hard on his lead again.

During our conversation, Amadeus told me many other things that made my heart bleed. The cruelty that had been inflicted upon him was tremendous. He told me he wanted to stay always with Rhonda and never leave her for another home. He'd had several owners and was worried about moving again. I assured him that Rhonda would never leave him, and that he would never again be treated so cruelly. I also told him he was a very clever dog and that he would do well at the flyball competition.

I asked Rhonda to phone me the night before the competition so I could go over everything with Amadeus to remind him what he had to do. After the event, Rhonda called to say Amadeus had gone into the box, picked up his ball and behaved very well on the lead. He hadn't bitten any of the other dogs.

Things went well for a few weeks, then Rhonda called and asked me to speak to Amadeus again. The day before, he had finished the flyball competition and done everything right. He was walking away when suddenly, for no apparent reason, he went after another dog and bit it. Rhonda was upset because the other dog's vet bill had cost her $200.

I tuned into Amadeus and he told me he didn't want the other dogs coming near him after he'd finished, and that's why he went for them. I told him that was very unkind, and that he must not attack the other dogs; otherwise he would be removed from the team and would not be allowed to compete again. I told him Rhonda would keep him apart from the other dogs as best she could.

Before the next competition, Rhonda called and asked me to remind Amadeus not to attack the other dogs. I tuned into Amadeus and suddenly I felt great sadness and worry. I asked him what was wrong and he told me one of their cats was very sick and was dying. Amadeus wanted to know where the cat would go if it died. I often find when animals have been abused they equate dying with going to another cruel home. I reassured him, and told him that dying meant the cat's spirit would go to another place where he would be very happy. I explained how when the body wears out and feels pain, then the spirit must leave the worn-out body and move on. That's what dying is, I told him.

Rhonda confirmed that one of the cats was sick. I told her Amadeus was really too upset to talk at that point because unlike humans, animals can think of only one thing at a time. The cat's illness had made Amadeus too preoccupied to allow effective communication. This was not the day to speak to him; he needed a week or so to get over it.

A few weeks later I was able to talk to Amadeus again and I told him how much it upset Rhonda when he attacked the other dog. Amadeus told me he didn't like the smell of the other dog, so he bit him. I told him it made Rhonda sad when he misbehaved and was unkind to other dogs. Amadeus wanted to do everything correctly. He wanted to work closely with Rhonda and he wanted to get the course right. I reassured him he was a beautiful clever dog, much too smart to bite other dogs. He agreed he would behave in the future and there have been no further problems since that time.

I often find that when people have rescued pets, problems crop up that relate to incidents in the animal's early life, before the current owner came along. It takes a lot of love and patience to determine the origin of these leftover problems, but like any other difficulty with animal behaviour, if we can put ourselves in the place of the animal and try to look at things from its point of view, often we can hit upon the proper solution.

These are some of the ways in which animals can misbehave when they are feeling neglected or misunderstood. Next, I will tell you about the problem that makes pet owners most unhappy, when an animal that was once trained begins to have accidents or does not use the litter box. Litter box and soiling problems are among the most difficult challenges pet owners face, but there are always reasons for such difficulties, as we shall see in the next chapter.

CHAPTER 4

Litter Box Blues: house-breaking and litter problems

Nothing is more upsetting to pet owners than animals that have problems with house-breaking or using the litter box. It is bad enough having to scoop and wipe and scrub every time you turn around, but when you consider the damage to your home, carpet, furniture and clothing, such accidents can cost a tremendous amount of money.

All these difficulties combine to make house-breaking and litter box mishaps among the leading reasons people seek my advice. The problem is especially unsettling when a pet that has been house-trained suddenly starts soiling. I always find that the animal has a good reason for these 'accidents'; usually it is their way of communicating their displeasure with a particular situation that has developed in their home. Only rarely does a medical condition turn out to be the cause.

I also find the problem is more frequent with cats. Sometimes it may take a while to get a puppy completely house-broken, but once they are, they don't generally have accidents unless they are ill or are left unattended for too long. Cats, however, are very sensitive when it comes to their litter boxes, and changes we may consider insignificant can throw them completely. Often, too, cats show their disapproval of a particular situation by relieving themselves outside their box.

It is important to remember that animals vary in their habits just as children do. Some puppies learn within a matter of months, while others may need up to a year before they really understand that they must perform their bodily functions outside the house. By the same token, some dogs may go immediately after being taken outside, while others must sniff every bush for a mile before finding a suitable location.

You must be patient with your dog's or cat's particular style. Remember that we humans always have a bathroom nearby, while animals must rely on us to determine when they need to go outside. Some owners are negligent about taking their pet out frequently enough, then become angry with an animal that has soiled after being confined to an apartment for hours on end with no break. I had a client whose grown dog was soiling during the day. But when I visited I learned that the lady did not let the poor dog out all day long. Once again, it was the owner who was at fault, not the pet.

According to the American Veterinary Association, this type of problem is the main reason why pets are given up for adoption by their families, and also the number one explanation given by families asking a vet to put down an animal that is not ill.

I abhor the idea of a pet being put down simply because of a house-training problem. It breaks my heart when animals are penalized simply because their owners have failed to shoulder the responsibilities of pet ownership.

Animals must be trained to do what you want them to do, and the training must be done with love, compassion and a great deal of patience.

Still, I understand how upsetting accidents can be to owners. We all want our homes to be pleasant and comfortable, and constant wetting will ruin a carpet. There comes a point when the smell of pet urine reaches down into the carpet underlay and simply cannot be removed. Then you have no choice but to replace the carpet or live with the unpleasant smell. Defecation presents its own problems. If the animal is regular, scooping up the mess presents little difficulty. But if it is suffering from loose bowels, a permanent stain can result.

Clients often ask me why their animal is having accidents. Such difficulties are never the animal's fault, but can always be traced back to something the owner is doing or not doing which is upsetting to the pet. House-training accidents are one sure way in which your pet can grab your attention. In the case of neglected pets, they would much rather have the negative attention that comes with the scolding over the accident than none of your attention at all.

With a bit of observation and perhaps even a little detective work, you can almost always discover the reason your pet is soiling, and then take appropriate steps to remedy the problem.

As with all pet problems, there are logical reasons for the accidents. Many times a change in the home or the family is responsible. Often the problem can be something as simple as a change in diet, litter or the location of the litter box, which upsets and confuses the animal and takes it out of its usual routine.

If you can think back over the week preceding the start of the accidents, try to isolate anything different in your pet's routine. Have you changed its food or schedule, or bought it a new dish? Is there a new animal (or human baby) in the house? Has a family member been ill or away? Has there been unusual stress or discord in your home? Have you been overworked and unable to give your pet its normal share of attention?

Animals can react very badly when they sense that their humans are upset, and one of the first ways their own unhappiness often manifests itself is with a soiling accident. It is an animal's way of raising a red flag and saying, 'I don't like what is going on here.'

Animals know soiling is not desirable behaviour; that is why they often try to hide their misdeeds. Pets love their humans and want more than anything to please them, so you can be sure if an animal is deliberately engaging in a behaviour it knows will upset you, it is for what it considers to be a very good reason.

We must also remember that animals, just like humans, have different personalities. We tend to think, 'Well, this is what I want my pet to do, so he must do it,' without making any allowances for the animal's individual preferences. For example, there are some people who think nothing of drying off with a towel someone else has just used, while others would never do that. Animals also have their peculiarities and we must make allowances for those. In a multi-cat household, some cats will use a litter box all the other cats are using; but many cats absolutely will not.

Cats are very clean animals and it is important to them to have a clean place to perform their bodily functions. If you are negligent about keeping their litter tray fresh and scooped out, don't be surprised if your cat finds another place to go to the bathroom. You must stop this tendency immediately, because once a cat decides on a place to use as its bathroom, it is difficult to change its mind. You must train your kitten to go where you want it to go, and be diligent about keeping the litter tray clean, so as not to give your cat the idea it must go elsewhere.

The same is true of litter box location. Cats are creatures of habit. You may decide to move the litter box because it suits you, but the cat is used to having it where it has always been and will more than likely continue going to the bathroom in its accustomed spot, whether or not the litter tray is there. While some cats don't mind a change of location and will follow their litter box around, you would be surprised how many cat owners call me with complaints about accidents who answer yes to my first question, 'Have you just moved the litter box?' If they answer yes, I tell them simply to move the litter box back to where it was, no matter how inconvenient it may seem, and this solves the soiling problem.

Also, don't shut your cat in to too close a space. I have had many clients consult me about litter box problems who have followed the current trend and bought fancy domed litter boxes. Though the dome may keep litter from spraying, it tends to make some cats feel claustrophobic, while others don't mind the enclosed space at all. In cases where the cat started avoiding the litter tray once the dome appeared, all the soiling problems were resolved once the owners removed the dome from the litter box and gave their cats a little breathing space.

Animals are very vulnerable when they are doing their business, so they tend to be more jumpy at this time. Just recently a friend's cat, a wise old veteran of fifteen years, was relieving himself in the back garden early one morning. He let his guard down for a moment, and there, in the middle of a suburban neighbourhood, a fox jumped out of the hedge, grabbed the cat, and broke its neck before my friend could chase it away. So try to be a bit more understanding if your pet doesn't like to perform in the open.

Once you have determined what factors may have altered in the week preceding the change in behaviour, you can formulate a plan to try to eliminate the cause of the accidents. It may take a bit of time to solve the problem, but your pet is worth it. If you find you really cannot get the problem corrected, you may decide to allow the animal to live outdoors as long as you have a spacious, secure and sheltered place for him. If you do not, it is your responsibility to try to find a good home for your pet. Having a pet put down because it is having accidents is entirely unacceptable, and most vets of my acquaintance will not do it. But they tell me they get many requests for such services from pet owners who thought the fluffy little kitten or adorable puppy was just going to take care of itself without any training or input from the owners at all.

Neither animals nor children can grow up properly by themselves, so if you do not think you can make the commitment of time, love and energy it takes to turn an animal into a proper pet, it is just as well if you don't get a pet at all. You will save yourself a lot of trouble and some dog or cat a lot of heartbreak. If, however, you are willing to make the effort of training your pet to be a good companion, please continue reading, and I will share some stories of pets whose soiling problems I was able to correct.

Misty

I had an unusual case presented to me by my client, Kerry. Whenever she was at home, her cat, Misty, used the litter box consistently. But when Kerry went out, the cat used the rest of the house as a sort of giant litter box. Needless to say, neither Kerry nor her family were pleased with this turn of events.

At first I thought it was just a case of Misty being spoiled and wanting her mistress to stay home all the time, a situation which can often be remedied by the addition of another cat to keep the first cat company (see the story of Whiskey in Chapter 5). But once I connected telepathically to the cat, I came to understand that Misty had experienced a tremendous fright months before while still a kitten. Kerry was away from the house and just as Misty was entering her litter box, she heard a tremendous crash of thunder and saw a bright lightning flash. Misty associated the terrifying boom with two things: her attempt to use the litter box and Kerry's absence. Whenever Kerry was around to protect her, Misty felt it was safe to use the litter box. But once she left the house, the cat was afraid the thunder would return if she tried to use the box.

I told Misty it was all right, that the same thing was not likely to happen again, and that the thunder and lightning could not hurt her while she was in the house. To give Misty a sense of control and empowerment, something she sorely lacked, I asked where she wanted her litter tray placed. Misty answered that if it could go in the cupboard where she liked to sleep, it would feel safe to her in there.

When I told Kerry about the thunder and lightning, she confirmed there had been a big storm several months previously when she was away from home. When she returned that evening, she found Misty cowering in her cupboard, and the litter box problems began the very next day. Kerry said that Misty spent most of her time hiding in the cupboard and many of the accidents occurred there.

Now we had the key to the origin of the problem, but I was concerned when Kerry told me about Misty hiding out all the time because occasional thunder and lightning did not seem to me to be enough of a reason for the cat to be so frightened. I decided to wait and see what would happen. Sure enough, after Kerry moved Misty's litter tray to the cupboard as requested, the cat went without a problem for a few weeks.

Then Kerry called me again. Misty was once more having problems, even with the litter box in the requested location. When I connected to the cat again, I asked her what else was going on that was frightening her and making her have accidents. She was very hesitant about talking to me, but after much prodding, she told me her daddy, Kerry's husband, had been throwing his shoes at her when she was hiding in the cupboard and deliberately hitting her with them. His anger frightened her so badly she lost control of her bowels and had an accident, which enraged him even more. Misty was so terrified of Kerry's husband that she hid in the cupboard whenever he was in the house, but he had discovered her hiding place, and seemed to enjoy cruelly teasing the poor animal.

It is always difficult for me to have to tell a client that one of their family members is abusing their pet, and that this is the source of their animal's difficulties. You can imagine what an impossible situation it puts my clients in when they confront the miscreant with the information. The abuser always demands to know who 'told' on them. It is hard to explain to someone who is not sympathetic to animals that the animal itself 'told'.

Of course, I could not tell Kerry to choose between her cat and her husband, but that is often what I would like to tell people. When I find out from animals that their owner's spouse or sweetheart is being cruel, I want to shout, 'You will never be happy with someone who does not love animals as you do.'

Kerry tearfully confirmed what Misty had told me, and said that her husband disliked the cat, particularly since it had started soiling, and often threw his shoes at it. I told her she had to protect her cat from her husband, and if she could not, then she must find another home for it.

Sadly, Kerry called several months later to say she had had Misty put down. Her husband had given her an ultimatum and she gave in. If she had just taken the trouble to find a new home for Misty, I know the difficulties would have cleared up. All the poor cat needed was a home filled with love and compassion. She was so frightened that she rarely left her cupboard. Though it is sad that Kerry chose to sacrifice her cat, it comforts me to know Misty is in a better place now where she will not suffer any more.

Misty's case, though complicated by the abuse, is not unusual in that I have worked with many animals who were particularly sensitive to electrical storms. Storms are extremely upsetting for some animals, while others sleep peacefully through the worst thunder and lightning. It has to do with the individual animal's sensitivity to the earth's electromagnetic fields. If an animal is very sensitive, electrical storms can actually cause it physical pain. I have felt it in my own body when I am linked telepathically to a sensitive animal. It is not just the noise of the thunder; there is much more going on. A sensitive animal serves as an electrical conduit when storms are nearby, and as you can imagine, this is terribly frightening for them. Think of how you jump in the winter when you touch metal after building up a static electrical charge. The same thing happens to animals.

Be aware of what your animal may be experiencing. Just because you cannot feel anything, don't assume your animal cannot. Our bodies don't operate at the same electrical frequencies as animal bodies, therefore our senses are not as attuned as theirs to changes in the electromagnetic fields.

I have found that some animals can feel the electrical impulses from a human body as well. If you approach them too quickly, this will cause them discomfort, so please be aware that this may be what is causing a dog or cat to pull back from you. It's not that they are unfriendly; they are simply trying to protect themselves from your electrical charge. If you have a pet that reacts to people in this way, just tell your guests to ignore him. He will come around in his own time and own way, when he feels comfortable about doing so.

If you know your animal is sensitive to electricity, try not to leave him alone during a storm, and especially avoid leaving him outside. If your pet wants to go under a bed during a storm, let him. It will help him to feel safe, and the stillness and the enclosed space will guard against the build-up of a static charge. The fright your animal feels after experiencing an electric shock may cause him to lose control of his bowels or bladder, so be particularly sympathetic if you find your pet has soiled on a stormy day.

Sparky

Celia came to me because her dog, Sparky, had taken to making a daily deposit near her new boyfriend's shoes and clothes after he left them on the floor by the bedside. Her boyfriend had ordered Celia to get rid of the dog or he himself would depart, but she didn't want to lose either her human or her canine companion.

Celia and Sparky had been together for ten years, ever since Sparky was a puppy. Celia said the beautiful Dalmatian had never had an accident in all that time, so I suspected that Sparky was either jealous of the attention his mistress was paying her new boyfriend, or didn't like the boyfriend and had fallen back on an age-old device to show his disapproval.

When I connected telepathically to the dog, I found Sparky was greatly distressed because he thought the boyfriend treated him unkindly. He was also, as I suspected, jealous, and did not like having the man living in the house because he was used to having Celia all to himself. He missed their evening romps and was desperate for a bit of Celia's attention. Sparky was lonely and afraid. He was used to sleeping in Celia's bedroom every night and now found himself shut out, replaced by the unsympathetic boyfriend who kicked him and treated him cruelly whenever Celia was out and he was alone with the dog. The dog told me the man had threatened to hurt him repeatedly, and taunted him by saying he would get rid of him sooner or later.

Celia was worried about her dog and didn't want him to feel entirely neglected, so she had started letting him into the bedroom early each morning. Sparky seized upon this as a prime opportunity to show his disapproval of the boyfriend by performing his bodily functions on or near the man's shoes and on his clothing, something which he had never done before. He emphasized to me that he had always been a clean dog and his bodily functions were regular, so I knew the 'accidents' were deliberate. When I asked Sparky why he was soiling, he told me he repeated this behaviour most mornings hoping Celia would under-stand why he was doing it.

But, of course, she didn't. Her heart and emotions were tied up with the new boyfriend and she couldn't understand why her reliable old pet had suddenly started misbehaving. Her boyfriend was enraged and had issued the standard 'It's him or me' ultimatum.

I wouldn't have any difficulty making such a choice; the pet would always win. If you are an animal lover, it is important that your partner loves animals, too, or you will surely face problems ahead.

Though Sparky had excellent reasons for his misdeeds, I never encourage pets to continue misbehaving because it only serves to aggravate an already tense situation. When I told Celia that Sparky had told me her boyfriend treated him badly, I gently pointed out that she could never be truly happy with someone who was not as great an animal lover as she was. I told her she had to take steps to protect Sparky from her boyfriend and make him feel as special to her as he did before the boyfriend came into her life. Then and only then would the accidents stop.

Not surprisingly, that was not the answer Celia wanted to hear, so she left my studio. Somehow, she expected me to wave a magic wand and cure all her difficulties. But as all my clients soon discover, they have to work at resolving their problems with their animals. There are no easy cures.

I hoped for the best, but felt that poor Sparky had seen his last happy days. I knew he wasn't going to stop his accidents because he was trying to make a point. I was afraid Celia would get rid of her old friend.

But there was a happy ending this time. Three months later, Celia returned unexpectedly and told me she had finally broken up with her male companion. It turned out her dog's opinion of her suitor was the correct one; it just took her a bit longer than it took Sparky to figure it out. The man had been gone just a week, and Sparky was still making his daily deposits in the spot where once the man had thrown his clothes. Celia wanted me to speak to Sparky to assure him the boyfriend would not be coming to live in the house again.

I connected to the dog and gave him the happy news, and Celia has since reported that Sparky is now accident-free once again. Celia learned something from the experience and has decided she will never get serious about a man again before determining whether or not he loves animals.

Another lady came to me because her three dogs were having accidents on her carpet, a problem which had developed since the introduction of a fourth dog into the household. We solved her problem, but not until we had sorted out the hurt feelings and fears of abandonment the three older dogs experienced as a result of the new dog's presence in their home. Since accidents are often the result of jealousy and upset over the presence of a new animal, I will present solutions for this problem in the next chapter.

CHAPTER 5

Living in harmony and love: introducing new animals to the household

Pet owners often run into unexpected trouble when a new pet is brought into the household. The introduction of a new animal can wreak havoc upon a formerly quiet domestic scene. It upsets the pecking order of the animals already in the home, and everything must be sorted out before peace can reign again. It is most important that the pets you already have do not feel displaced by the newcomer. At the same time, you must make sure the newcomer does not get left out and feels truly welcome in your home. It is a delicate balance to achieve.

On the other hand, sometimes the addition of a new animal solves problems that may be related to loneliness, depression or skittishness on the part of a solitary animal. If you work long hours and leave your pet alone, loneliness may lead him into mischief. The addition of another animal to a situation like this will often relieve the unhappiness of the solitary pet and put an end to the behavioural problems.

Pet owners are making a big mistake when they bring new animals into the house without informing the animals already in residence that a newcomer is arriving. I tell all my clients never to assume their pets do not have a point of view about additions to the family, because they do. I stress the importance of communicating the news to your animals *before* the new animal arrives. Ask their permission to bring another pet in. It may seem silly, but including your pet in the decision-making process by discussing his new role with him ahead of time prevents many problems.

Emphasize how much you love your pet, and how big a role he plays in your family. This is very important, as one of their greatest fears is that the newcomer may oust them from their favoured place. Like a child who reacts badly to the birth of a sibling, an older pet may feel shoved aside by a newer, younger and possibly more beautiful animal's arrival in the home he once considered his alone. No matter what, a newcomer inevitably alters the balance of power among the animals. You should be sensitive to your pet's feelings and make sure you give him his accustomed shows of affection. If you fail to spend time with your older pets after a new pet arrives, your old pets are likely to blame the newcomer for the neglect and problems will result.

The stress and conflict associated with the introduction of a new animal can actually cause your pet to become ill. That is what happened with Zuki, an iguana that was brought to me at the point of death.

Zuki

Since I started healing animals, I have worked with many different types of creatures, dogs and cats of course, but also birds, horses and turtles. But Zuki was my first iguana.

Zuki arrived in my studio concealed in a duffel bag. He

had been so ill his owner, Karen, was afraid to open the
bag because she thought he might already be dead. When
I lifted him from the bag, he was limp and completely
unresponsive, yet my first thought was that he was one of
the most beautiful creatures I had ever seen. Neither Karen
nor a succession of veterinarians had been able to discover
what was wrong with him. Zuki would not eat, and had
grown progressively more lethargic over the previous ten
days.

I put a soft, clean towel across my lap, lifted the iguana
out of the bag and put him down on the towel. Zuki was
still a baby, not more than eighteen inches long and less
than two years old. As always, I took a few minutes to feel
the animal's energy and get it used to me. As I stroked
Zuki, I told the iguana what I was doing and asked his
permission to help him. I waited until I felt my healing
guide put the healing energy through my hands, then I put
my hands gently upon him and stroked his head.

I started to get a sensation of extreme discomfort in my
stomach, and felt there was a blockage in the iguana's
intestinal area. I was given a blue light to use and drew it
from the tip of Zuki's nose to the tip of his tail, all the
while visualizing the healing light going through him. I
realized my guide was going to have me perform psychic
surgery. I then visualized using the laser to cut Zuki's
stomach open, and I could see that it was quite sore inside.
I put more healing energy through his stomach, then saw
the energy clearing the blockage and going through Zuki.
I closed the stomach, rested my hands on the iguana, and
felt vibrations in my hands as healing energy passed through
them. After another ten minutes of healing, the iguana

passed the intestinal blockage onto the towel, and I was very happy I had thought to cover myself before picking Zuki up!

I continued to heal Zuki until I felt energy flowing freely through him. After being listless and still for more than a week, the iguana suddenly started to move and his eyes were brighter. Karen couldn't believe the iguana had recovered so quickly, and thought it was nothing short of a miracle. She was overjoyed to see Zuki so active, especially when he indicated he wanted to climb down and explore the studio.

I was curious to see if I could communicate easily with the iguana; I wondered if he was as observant and intelligent as the rest of the animals I worked with. He did not disappoint me. As Zuki continued to improve, he began to communicate rapidly.

As animals often do when they are feeling better and realize they have an audience, Zuki started to gossip about his family. He told me Karen's daughter, Shannen, had just changed her hair. When I relayed this, Karen said it was true. Zuki also told me he had been moved from Shannen's bedroom into another room, and he wished to go back as he enjoyed the feeling of companionship he shared with Shannen, who was his special favourite in the family.

Zuki then told me he had been given something horrible to eat. Karen thought for a moment, then said it was tofu. Zuki promptly told me he didn't want any more of that, that iguanas didn't eat tofu, and Karen agreed not to offer it any more. Zuki then returned to his favourite topic, Shannen, and told me when he lived in her room he used to enjoy watching her. He said she often read in bed and

that her bedroom was very untidy, which made her mother
cross. 'Absolutely true!' Karen cried out.

Zuki also said the girl often left her mug and plates at
the side of the table. He couldn't understand why Karen
got angry over this. He couldn't see that it mattered, and
thought it was strange to get angry over something like
that. He kept emphasizing how much he wanted to go back
into the bedroom with Shannen, who he said talked to him
all the time and made him feel special and important.

By this time, we were all laughing out loud and Zuki
was getting perkier and perkier. I had never seen such a
remarkable recovery. He told me our conversation had made
him feel much happier.

Then Zuki really began to open up. He told me there
was another iguana in his house who had been cruel to
him. I suddenly picked up the other animal, named Spika,
who started to talk. I was amazed at the intensity of the
creature's jealousy towards little Zuki. Spika did not like
Zuki at all and proceeded to tell me in no uncertain terms
he wanted Zuki to die and go away. I realized part of
Zuki's illness was caused by the stress of the other iguana's
intense jealousy. Karen, from her human point of view,
thought the two iguanas would enjoy being close to each
other. On the contrary, I found the animals disliked
each other intensely.

The main source of trouble turned out to be a glass
enclosure which had originally been Spika's. Spika had
outgrown the enclosure and had been given a splendid new
cage to accommodate his size. Karen had then given Spika's
old cage to Zuki.

But to Spika's way of thinking, his favourite cage had

been thoughtlessly taken away without regard to his feelings. It didn't matter that he could hardly fit in the cage any longer. He couldn't see it from the standpoint of practicality. Spika felt only intense jealousy, because he believed he had been unfairly removed from his cage so that Zuki could have it. I also discovered Spika did not like to share the attention his family had formerly lavished solely upon him.

When Karen placed the two cages in the same room, Spika took advantage of their proximity to torment poor Zuki. Zuki felt intimidated by the older iguana, and completely subject to his power. The strong negative energy vibrations Spika constantly sent Zuki's way were actually what had made the little iguana ill.

I'm sure you've all heard of voodoo. What Spika did to Zuki was comparable to that ancient practice; he made Zuki believe he was going to become ill and die, and the power of that suggestion made Spika's heartfelt wish become Zuki's unhappy reality. He really believed it when the other iguana told him he didn't want him there and that he was dying.

I told Karen to separate the iguanas' cages so they could not see each other, which would put Zuki well away from Spika's negative energy vibrations. I asked her to put Zuki's cage back with the daughter who loved him, as he had always enjoyed the girl's company in the past. Karen readily agreed, so I reassured Zuki he would not have to see the other iguana again, which made him very happy.

The intense jealousy Spika directed constantly at the little iguana had broken down Zuki's immune system, making him vulnerable to illness, and more and more despondent. The joy of hearing he would not ever have to see his jealous rival again proved the best medicine of all for Zuki.

Back into the duffel bag went Zuki, now happy and healthy, for the journey home. As he was settling down, he poked his head up one last time and asked me to have Karen raise the temperature in his tank as he liked it a bit warmer. I promised I would tell her. When Zuki returned home, his tank was immediately moved back into Shannen's room. Karen reports that Zuki happily watches Shannen for hours on end.

Much of this difficulty could have been avoided by communicating with Spika prior to Zuki's introduction to the household. There is no doubt in my mind Spika would still have been jealous, because that was part of his personality. But it would have lessened the intensity of his angry feelings if he had been reassured beforehand about his ongoing role in the family, his importance and the love the family had for him. It did soothe Spika somewhat when I told him the reason his cage had been taken from him and given to Zuki was not a punishment as he had supposed or to show favouritism to Zuki, but simply to accommodate his growth. But I suspect Spika will always be jealous of Zuki.

Hubert

After several idyllic years as Stacey's fondest companions, my old friends Hubert and Leonard, introduced in Chapter 3, found themselves in charge of two young kittens. Because their owner Stacey had asked their permission to bring the kittens into the house, they did not feel jealous or cause any problems. But there is still a funny story to be told here, a story that illustrates the wisdom of including your pets in the decision to add new animals to your home.

The funny part is about Hubert. As we already know, Hubert is highly strung and quite stubborn. We could rarely make him give up a bad habit unless we showed him how he could benefit from acquiescing to our request. But when confronted with parental responsibility, Hubert did an about-face. He decided to give up his old ways and become a perfect role model for the kitties.

Stacey had bought a nice scratching post which Hubert steadfastly refused to use, much preferring to sharpen his claws on his favourite spot on Stacey's sofa. We had made little progress towards a resolution of this problem despite several conversations with Hubert. But after I told him he must set a good example for the new kittens and show them how to behave properly, Hubert became a new cat. He took his role very seriously, and Stacey reported he could be seen stretching and exercising his claws on the scratching post whenever the kittens came near – the perfect adult feline role model. No more sofa-scratching for Hubert, and certainly none for the kittens in his charge.

The next time I connected to Hubert through Stacey's energy, I congratulated him on his progress towards responsibility. He told me that once he found himself in charge of teaching the kittens the right way to behave, he realized he himself couldn't be seen behaving badly, and so he changed his old habits accordingly.

I like Hubert's story because it is a good example of the positive things that can happen when a new animal is properly introduced to a multi-pet household. When you take pains to make sure your old pets still feel loved and important, and emphasize to them that the newcomer will serve only to make the family even happier, you can stop problems before they start.

Murphy

My client Pam took no such precautions. She brought a beautiful new dog into her home without thinking of the effect it might have on the dog she already had. Her family showered such lavish attention on the newcomer that their old dog felt quite left out. When he started to attack the new dog in an attempt to draw some attention back to himself, the poor dog found it had quite the opposite effect from what he desired. His formerly loving family turned on him for being cruel to the new dog. What they didn't understand was that the attacks were his way of expressing his dismay at their almost total neglect of him.

My involvement in the story began when Pam came to me and said she'd had to drop her dog Murphy off at a vet's surgery, where the animal was being boarded for the day while Pam was in Houston. I asked her why she needed to take Murphy to the vet's if she was going to be away only for the day. Pam said it was because Murphy kept attacking her other dogs, and he was in a terrible state with all his hair coming out. He was almost bald.

I felt an overwhelming sense of compassion for Murphy, so I asked Pam if she would like me to see if I could tune in to Murphy and find out why he was attacking the other dogs. I explained to Pam that there always had to be a reason for an animal's misbehaviour, and that perhaps I could help her sort out the problems with the dogs in her household.

Without questioning me further, Pam said yes, she would appreciate any help she could get with the problem as it was causing great distress in her family.

When I connected to Murphy through Pam's energy, a very sad little voice came through, and I realized the dog was terribly upset. He told me he was broken-hearted because his family was going to give him away. When I relayed this to Pam, she looked at me absolutely astonished and said she'd only just asked her maid that morning if she would take Murphy, because the maid loved Murphy very much, and Pam was fed up with the problems that Murphy was causing. I explained to Pam that animals understand everything we are saying. Still, the remark made that morning was the result of weeks of Murphy's misbehaviour, so I hadn't got to the bottom of the mystery yet.

Murphy then told me that Pam's daughter had called him ugly. That made him sad because once he had been a beautiful dog, but as his hair had mostly fallen out, he knew he wasn't beautiful any more. Hearing Pam's daughter call him ugly just added to his pain.

When I told Pam this, she said, 'Oh, we do call him ugly, but only as a joke! We didn't realize he knew what we meant!' Pam was devastated at the hurt the family's unthinking joke had caused her little dog. She went on to tell me that Murphy was the family's first dog, and she'd always had a special fondness for him before the trouble started.

Murphy interrupted to say his family had had him before any other dogs came into the house, and that he had always felt beautiful and special. Then Pam decided to add to her dog family. She bought two more dogs, and the new dogs had puppies, including one with soft fur and beautiful eyes they called Charlotte. Pam decided to keep Charlotte in addition to her other three dogs.

Soon after, Murphy began to feel neglected. He felt all the attention was on Charlotte, whereas it used to be on him. Learning to share the affection of their masters can be just as difficult for animals as it is for human brothers and sisters, particularly when they have been the centre of attention for some time before the newcomer appears.

Murphy told me that Charlotte and her mother and father would not speak to him at all, and this made him feel very sad and lonely. Murphy started attacking Charlotte, and the attacks had grown so vicious that Pam was forced to separate the two dogs. Pam was at a loss as to what caused the trouble, since the dogs had been getting along beautifully when first introduced.

I asked Murphy why he was attacking Charlotte when he knew it distressed his family and made them angry with him. He replied that everyone thought Charlotte was beautiful and he wasn't beautiful any more because his hair was falling out, so he was jealous. Murphy also told me the other dogs had much nicer dishes to eat from.

When I told Pam what Murphy was saying, she started crying. She told me she didn't think it mattered what dish a dog ate from and was amazed that Murphy perceived the difference between his plain plastic bowl and the other dogs' special stainless steel dog dishes. She hadn't realized that a dog could interpret such a thing as a sign of preferential treatment and favouritism.

I told Pam all of Murphy's undesirable behaviour stemmed from his need for attention from his family, attention he felt he was no longer getting since the arrival of Charlotte. The family was naturally cross with him for attacking Charlotte, not realizing that Murphy was so unhappy and that it was the only way he knew to let his family and the other dogs know how he was feeling. He was getting his family's attention, even if it was the wrong kind of attention. Murphy was crying out to be loved.

Pam also had to put Murphy into a room by himself so he couldn't attack the other dogs, which only added to Murphy's distress because he felt lonely and upset at being shut away from his beloved family. I told Pam that instead of shutting Murphy away all the time, it should be used as a punishment when he attacked Charlotte. I instructed her to say very firmly to him, 'No! You don't do that to Charlotte,' and then put him in a room alone for about ten minutes every time he attacked, so he would realize the undesirable confinement was the direct result of his undesirable behaviour, instead of believing the confinement was his family's way of shutting him out because they didn't love him any more.

The sadness and upset Murphy was transmitting to me was disturbing, particularly because I knew the dog's distress was caused by his family's misunderstanding of the situation. I reassured Pam that many pet owners would have responded in the same way and asked her what she wanted to do. Pam said she wanted to keep Murphy, that she loved him very much, and had only suggested giving him away

because she didn't know what else to do. I told her that I
would speak to the dog and convey her love, but that she
had to make the changes I suggested if she expected Murphy
to show any improvement. Pam agreed.

I spoke to Murphy and assured him that Pam and his
family still loved him very much, and that there was no
reason for him to attack Charlotte again because everyone
loved him as much as they loved Charlotte. I told him I
knew he would be a very good dog now, and that even
though I understood why he had felt so very jealous, there
was no need any longer for that sort of behaviour.

Murphy then asked about his hair. He was worried that
he had been pumped so full of steroids, in an effort to
cure the inflammatory condition that had caused the hair
loss, that his fur would never grow back. I heard my angel
guides saying that he should be on a diet of rice and fresh
fish; then his hair would grow again. I told Pam about the
special diet, and reminded her to get Murphy a new stainless
steel dish. I then told Murphy he was going to get his own
special bowl like the other dogs had.

Pam called my studio a few days later to tell me that
everything was much better. Murphy had his new dish, and
lots of love and reassurance from his suddenly cognizant
family. Everyone in the family was telling him how beautiful
he was.

Pam also reported that Murphy was getting along much
better with the other dogs. While Pam was on the phone,
I tuned in to Murphy, and he transmitted to me a good
happy feeling; then he telepathically sent me a picture of
him sleeping together with the other dogs. I also picked
up another of Pam's dogs who told me that Murphy was

a nice dog again. I was very pleased that the dogs were communicating with each other, and that Murphy and his companions were all living in harmony once more.

A few weeks later, Pam brought Murphy to see me, and he had grown back a full coat of hair and was once again a beautiful dog. I could feel the pride and happiness flowing from him. Murphy had been re-established in an important role with his family, and now he regularly receives outward shows of love and affection. This was all he needed to correct both his behavioural and health problems.

Pam is still distraught over the pain her family's thoughtlessness caused Murphy, but it is common that we humans fail to realize that animals are such intelligent and sentient beings. Humans often don't give animals credit for their ability to understand.

As long as each pet feels special to its family, loved and appreciated, there should be no insurmountable problems. If real trouble begins after the introduction of a new animal, assess the time leading up to the difficulty and more often than not you will pinpoint the cause.

Whiskey

Sometimes a new animal can be just the right prescription to cure problems with a lonely, bored or skittish animal. The mingling of the two personalities often creates a more pleasant atmosphere for both the pet with the difficulties and for the family. The amusement and distraction provided by another animal can often take a neurotic animal's mind off his own problems and on to more agreeable occupations.

This was the case with my friend Carol. She came to
see me about her cat, Whiskey, who had taken to hiding
under the bed all day long. No matter what enticement
Carol presented, Whiskey would not come out from under
the bed in her bedroom upstairs. When I started to speak
with him, I discovered the ground floor of Whiskey's house
had taken in several feet of water during a devastating flood.
The family was forced to climb to the upper floor, and
they were caught there until the water subsided. The rising
waters, stormy weather and his family's upset had terrified
the poor cat.

After the disaster, the entire family had to live upstairs
while the ground floor was being repaired from the ravages
of the flood. The commotion of strange workmen trooping
in and out of the house all day, combined with the fearsome
noise of their power tools, had brought Whiskey to the
point of nervous collapse. One day he suddenly disappeared
under the bed, and now he wouldn't come out.

Through no one's fault, poor Whiskey had suffered so
many terrible experiences he could not cope with what had
happened. After so much trauma, the bed was the only
place, except for a nice dark cupboard, where he felt safe.
But sitting alone under the bed, Whiskey had too much
time to think about his troubles, so I suggested to him the
idea of a new kitten as a companion. I also asked Carol if
she had thought of getting a companion for Whiskey. She
said if it would help Whiskey, she would be in favour of
doing so.

As we communicated, I realized Whiskey was a very
chatty cat. He sent me lots of details about his owner's

clothes and appearance. He liked the idea of having another cat around and gave his approval.

The arrival of the new kitten was planned in detail with Carol, to make sure that Whiskey felt included in all the preparations. I warned him that the kitten was likely to be nervous after leaving its mother and might hiss a bit. But I assured Whiskey that if he took good care of the kitten they would become friends, and the friendship and amusement the kitten could provide would help take Whiskey's mind off his fear of another flood.

As we had hoped, the two cats did become friends, and once the curious little Samuel began to venture downstairs, Whiskey could not help but follow. This was a great breakthrough. By the end of the month, Carol reported that Whiskey and Samuel were living in all the rooms of the house. Whiskey's old terrors about being caught in another flood receded into his memory.

In Whiskey's case, the addition of Samuel to the household helped him overcome his fears and reclaim as his rightful territory all of his family's house.

No matter how difficult the situation, generally some resolution can be found to the problems caused by new animals. Answers, as always, lie in examining the changes in *human* conduct which led to the changes in the pet's conduct. If your old pet truly will not accept a newcomer, ask yourself why is it so important to bring a new animal home? Do you really need another pet? Can you provide for it properly, with nutritious food and good veterinary care? Do you have enough time to give a new pet the love and attention he needs? Or will the time you normally devote to the pets you already own have to be divided to accommodate all your animals, thereby knocking an established animal from its accustomed perch in the pecking order?

If you want to ensure a happy result when you introduce a new animal into your household, make sure the pets you already have feel included in the planning stage. Tell them that a new dog or cat is coming to live there and emphasize how much you love and appreciate them, and how you think the new arrival will be a wonderful addition to your family. Once the new pet arrives, make sure the newcomer isn't allowed to displace the pets you already have. If you make a fuss over the newcomer, take the time to make a fuss over your old friends, too, to keep jealous feelings at bay. If you are wise and don't allow a new pet to change your relationship with your old pet, such additions can go smoothly, resulting in increased satisfaction and pleasure for all those involved. Trouble will surely result, though, if you don't plan ahead, and ignore your old pets in favour of a new darling.

Sometimes, though, behavioural problems arise that are not due strictly to the introduction of a new animal. When owners inadvertently disrupt their pets' familiar environments, trouble can result. We discuss several examples in the next chapter.

CHAPTER 6

Sonny's proper schedule: the importance of routine

I cannot emphasize too strongly to pet owners the importance of establishing a routine with their animal and
sticking to it. With a reliable routine in place, pets are able
to overcome some of the more common traumas, such as
a change of house. To an animal which has no set routine,
such a move is completely unsettling, because the only
reliable thing in its life, its physical location, is suddenly
taken away. An animal which still has its familiar bed, dish
and toys, who is still enjoying its daily walk or romp with
its owners, will come through such a transition with far
fewer problems.

Though owners often come to see me about something
specific such as a soiling or fighting problem, frequently I
am able to trace the difficulty back to a change in their
routine, something which has upset or frightened their pet,
and resulted in the inappropriate behaviour. Pets are so very
like children. They need routine, discipline and structure
to stay on track, and when they do not get it, difficulties
of one sort or another often arise. I frequently discover
that a pet with significant behaviour problems has had
many different owners, or has suffered abuse. Many of these
problems can be overcome with the establishment of a
regular routine and lots of love. Once an animal has

a routine he can trust and a relationship with his owner he can depend upon, he is likely to drop many undesirable habits or neurotic behaviour patterns.

Your routine is one of the ways your animal tells time. Our pets know our daily routine and our weekend routine; that weekdays have a different rhythm from weekends. They understand the concept of 'day' and 'night' as light and darkness.

If you go to work at the same time each day and arrive home around the same time each night, that is a routine your pet depends on. But work schedules vary and we all have to work the occasional late night. It is important to let our pets know when we will be late, to keep them from worrying.

If you know you will be home late, try this exercise, because your pet will be expecting you and will be distressed if you don't show up on time. From your car or office, send a telepathic picture of darkness to tell your animal you are going to be home later than usual. Send the feeling of returning home later along with the words and the picture of darkness. Your message will reach your pet immediately, and he will know you'll be back later and not at your usual time. This will calm his fears about the break in the routine.

I have been consulted by people who were unsure how their pet knew exactly when to meet them even though their arrival time was different every day. One lady was especially puzzled. She was amazed by her dog barking to be let out into the garden a full ten minutes before her husband pulled up each night. Depending upon his workload, her husband's arrival times varied by as much as two hours, so she knew the time of day wasn't serving as the dog's cue. She wanted to know how their dog knew when the husband was on his way home.

The dog knew because the husband's mind energy was being transmitted telepathically as he commuted. I connected to the husband and discovered that while he was driving home, he sent out the feeling of pleasure he knew he would have upon arriving to find his happy family waiting for him. His intelligent and eager dog picked up this telepathic transmission immediately and barked to be let out into the garden so he could wait by the garage to greet his master and have his evening romp. It was clear to me that the husband's arrival home was an important part of this dog's daily routine. If something had disrupted his nightly jaunts to the garden, behavioural problems would have resulted.

As you plan your day, you think about where you have to go and when you have to be there. Unbeknown to you, all this information is transmitted telepathically to your animal, so they know you are about to leave the house, not only from the hustle and activity that precedes your departure, but also from the mental picture you have formed of going out to the car, starting the engine and driving away to your destination. In the same way, when you are returning, you transmit images of your arrival which your animal picks up. This is all part of your household routine.

If your animal is secure in his routine and knows he will be fed and walked regularly, played with, cared for and treated with great love and kindness, he is likely to experience few behavioural problems. An animal which has had no reliable care, endured thoughtless or cruel owners or

many owners, and suffered through many changes of
location, lives in a state of insecurity. There is nothing in
his life he can rely on, so he tends to distrust humans and
rely more upon himself. This often produces behavioural
problems since an independent animal sees little benefit in
co-operating with humans.

Sonny's Brass Horn

One of my cases involved a beautiful chestnut horse named
Brass, so named because his burnished coat glowed like the
brilliant metal. Gayle, his owner, called me because Brass
would not respond to his name or accept direction at all
when she rode him. He preferred to follow his own lead
and had taken Gayle on many wild and, occasionally, near-
calamitous rides. His favourite trick was to gallop full speed
under low-hanging branches. Gayle had a hard time trying
to stay in the saddle. When he was behaving, however, he
was a joy to ride, Gayle told me, with a satin-smooth gait
like a rocking horse.

If Gayle hadn't been a particularly capable and courageous
rider, she might have suffered serious injury. As we soon
discovered, Brass, though still a stallion, was not an uncon-
trollable horse, merely a headstrong one. He wasn't trying
to hurt Gayle, he just wanted to gain control over a situation
that was confusing and worrisome to him. Gayle was hoping
I could find out why Brass behaved as he did, and instil a
more co-operative spirit in the horse. She loved him dearly
and wanted to be able to trust him implicitly.

When I connected telepathically with Brass, he informed

me immediately and with great indignation that he would not respond to the name Brass because that was not his name at all — his name was Sonny, very much like my own nickname. After I told him Sunny was my name, he seemed to warm a bit. But this was where the initial confusion had come in. His first owner had named him Sonny's Brass Horn and called him Sonny, and he couldn't understand why his subsequent owners, and there had been many, insisted upon calling him Brass. He was adamant about this; Sonny was the only name he would answer to.

Then he told me he was very sorry about hurting Gayle's leg. When I told her this she was surprised because the injury had happened more than two years previously when Sonny had panicked and stumbled while jumping over a creek, accidentally knocking Gayle over and landing on her left leg.

Gayle asked me to reassure Sonny that she knew it was an accident, which greatly relieved the stallion. Sonny then told me his life had been a series of changes, going from one owner to the next and suffering cruel treatment at the hands of many. He told me one of his owners beat him with a stick, causing him to fall to his knees and injure his right leg, which hurt him still. He had been very frightened. He was trying to do what the man wanted him to do, but couldn't understand what was required of him because the man was so angry all the time. Sonny also told me he'd been tied up in a pen and beaten across the forehead and back, which fortunately did not cause him permanent physical injury. But the abuse had left psychological scars.

This saddened me greatly. I have found through working with horses that they often suffer horrendous abuse at the hands of their trainers or owners, beatings so severe they would kill a smaller animal. Is it any wonder that an animal which has been so badly abused would then turn against humans?

As horses are such large animals, they are capable of inflicting serious injury on humans. Trainers should keep this in mind before they raise their hand to strike a horse. A horse may tolerate such mistreatment for a short time, but when it decides it has had enough, the results can be quite deadly.

Though Gayle was a kind and loving person who handled Sonny gently, in her horse's experience humans were not to be trusted. Gayle was the first human he'd had contact with who hadn't abused him. He had been with Gayle over two years and made her unhappy on more than one occasion, yet she had never resorted to striking him. He wanted to know if he could continue to rely on her kindness, and I assured him he could.

Sonny was also tired of all the moves and disruptions in his life. He wanted a steady routine and had taken it upon himself to provide one. He did not feel he could rely on anything or anyone, not even the exceedingly patient and good-hearted Gayle, who treated Sonny with the only love and kindness he had ever known.

After talking to Sonny for a while, I understood his behavioural problems were a direct result of the lack of routine in his life, combined with all the abuse. Mistreatment and constant changes in his routine had made Sonny fearful, rebellious and not very willing to tolerate instruction from a human.

Sonny told me he loved Gayle very much, but they had

been through a hard time together. He was afraid she was going to get rid of him, and he would have to start all over again with a new owner. He didn't want that to happen, because he loved Gayle very much and thrived on all the attention she showered upon him. He also liked having his own pasture, where he could gallop to his heart's content.

When I explained this to Gayle, she confirmed her horse had a difficult past. At one time she had considered selling Sonny, but now was determined to work with him until he learned what was required. When I told Gayle how Sonny had been cruelly beaten so many times, she started to cry. She had no idea he had been so badly abused. She promised to start addressing Brass by his preferred name of Sonny, and told me she was beginning to understand why he was so stubborn and wilful, and so very skittish whenever a man approached him. In Sonny's experience, the arrival of a man meant a beating would soon follow.

After a time, Sonny had got used to Gayle's husband, Phil, who was as kind as Gayle. He allowed Phil to approach him in the stall or pasture without bolting. But all other men who came to work with Sonny, even if they were gentle, sent the stallion into a nervous state.

Sonny told me Phil was very worried Gayle would be seriously injured in a fall because of all the wild rides he had been giving her. He'd overheard Phil urging Gayle to sell him. I told this to Gayle and she said that Phil was indeed worried because of the ongoing problems with Sonny, but Gayle was determined to keep her horse and work through them. She wasn't worried about being hurt, because she knew the big stallion meant her no harm.

After speaking with Gayle, I assured Sonny he had a

permanent home with her. He would not be moved again.
I picked up a distinct love between Gayle and her horse,
and knew he wanted to please her, so I told Sonny he must
listen to Gayle, and do what she asked him to do. I
reminded him of the love Gayle showed him daily, and the
kind and thoughtful care she provided and would continue
to provide for him. He knew Gayle would not harm him
in any way, and I told him he could trust that feeling and
trust Gayle. But he had to mend his ways and take care of
Gayle when she rode him.

Gayle had said she was particularly worried about Sonny's
tendency to get out of control when they were in the forest.
He galloped full speed after other horses in the woods with
little regard for Gayle's safety. He sent me many pictures
of Gayle falling off his back and she confirmed it happened
more frequently than she liked, though it wasn't always
Sonny's fault. He then told me he always waited for Gayle
after she fell. Gayle confirmed this and said she considered
it quite a bonus. Otherwise she would have been in for
many long walks after taking a spill in the middle of
nowhere.

Interestingly, when I tried to talk to Sonny about the
importance of Gayle's safety, he moved away from the fence
and started eating grass, the picture of indifferent non-
chalance. I knew immediately that he didn't want to hear
this. He thought the chases in the forest were a game. He
loved stretching his legs and galloping full out to see if he
could overtake the other horses. He hadn't really been aware
of Gayle on his back, hanging on to her wildly charging
steed for her very life.

When I told Sonny his reckless behaviour was a big

problem for Gayle and that he had to be responsible for her safety when she was riding him, he moved back to the fence and started listening again. I told him he must pretend that he and Gayle were one and, therefore, had to move together. He couldn't go racing off wildly into the woods any more, endangering Gayle with his high-spirited play.

I also explained to Gayle that she could help by imagining herself inside Sonny's body and feeling herself to be a horse, with her arms as his front legs and her own legs as his back legs. This way she could telepathically transmit the behaviour she expected of him. If she wanted him to go slowly, she should imagine her own limbs moving slowly in a smooth, steady gait, and transmit that picture and feeling to Sonny. If she wanted him to halt, she should transmit that telepathically and Sonny would pick it up in his energy body and understand it much more quickly than any spoken command. If she could imagine herself to be one with the horse, the same as I had instructed Sonny, then they would learn to work together beautifully.

Gayle called the next day to say she'd had an interesting canter with Sonny that morning. She said his gait was slower and choppy, almost as if he was trying very hard to rein himself in and provide her with a safe ride. I told her that we would keep working with him to let him know what she wanted, and that she would have the horse of her dreams by the time we were finished.

When next I visited, I discovered a distinct pride in Sonny. He told me he was a beautiful horse, which he was, and that he was a good jumper and could move very fast. That love of speed was the very thing which was worrying Gayle, so I told Sonny he could gallop as fast as he liked when Gayle was not on his back, but that whenever she was in the saddle, he had to keep his speed down and listen to Gayle. He said he would try his best to do this, because he loved Gayle and Phil and wanted to please them. He was intelligent enough to realize the connection between his reckless behaviour and Phil's fears for Gayle's safety and was determined to do his part to keep Gayle safe on his back.

Though Sonny is still difficult at times, Gayle reports that his behaviour and responsiveness is steadily improving. She has learned she cannot expose Sonny to unfamiliar men because it stirs bad memories which in turn trigger bouts of inappropriate behaviour in the horse. She is careful to maintain Sonny's daily routine and not throw him any surprises, because his checkered past has left him with little ability to cope with unfamiliar situations, which he always interprets as threatening.

The establishment of a reliable routine has had a most beneficial effect in this situation. Whenever I communicate with Sonny, I find he is becoming more relaxed and secure in the permanence of his home with Gayle and Phil. Gayle is concentrating on developing her ability to communicate telepathically with Sonny, which pleases him immensely. Sonny and Gayle have developed an even deeper and more spiritual bond as a result of their telepathic communication.

Topaz

My client, Sylvia, called me from New York because she was having a problem paper-training her red miniature poodle, Topaz. Sylvia lived in an apartment in Manhattan. She had suffered through a year-long period of ill health, during which time she had mostly been confined to bed and hadn't been able to take Topaz out. She had been trying to teach him to relieve himself on papers in a tiled bathroom, where any spillover would be easy to clean up. But Topaz kept going in the hallway, which annoyed Sylvia's housemate, David. David was kind-hearted and had been trying to help Sylvia with the training, but they were not getting consistent results.

When I connected with Topaz, I discovered a very chatty, sociable dog, a real personality. I soon found the source of his confusion was the change in his routine. Before Sylvia became ill, he had been taken outside for walks, and encouraged to relieve himself there. When Sylvia could no longer take him out, Topaz couldn't understand what was required of him.

Topaz mentioned to me that he was a 'star'. I asked what he meant and he told me he went with David to entertain sick and housebound people as a clown dog. That gave me an idea. I told Topaz that stars didn't make messes in the hallway; that they always went on the paper in the bathroom.

I relayed to Sylvia what I had told Topaz and she confirmed that the dog had worked briefly with David. But the long hours away from her owner became difficult once Sylvia became ill. She decided to keep the dog home with her to relieve the monotony of her confinement. She loved the little dog dearly and his cheerful company took her mind off her illness. The only problem was with his paper training.

Topaz was proud he had been able to cheer Sylvia during

her illness and wanted to do whatever he could to help her. He promised me he would go on the paper, and stop wetting in the hall. But he hadn't finished talking, not by any means. He told me he liked his new red collar much better than his old one and enjoyed socializing when he went to the pet centre, where Sylvia sent him so he could play with other dogs. He also mentioned that he wished Sylvia would put his scarf back on. Sylvia was astounded when I told her that, because he'd only worn the scarf once, almost six months previously. Still, Topaz remembered the scarf and felt it made him look very beautiful. Sylvia laughed and told me she would have to initiate a search for the scarf as she couldn't quite remember where she'd put it.

Then Topaz bragged that his mummy took him to the 'beauty parlour' all the time and that made him even more beautiful than he already was. When I told this to Sylvia she laughed again, and confirmed that Topaz indeed enjoyed his regular visits to the groomer, where they doted on the charismatic little dog.

The next week, Sylvia reported that Topaz had started going on the paper immediately after I had talked to him, never missing. David couldn't believe it; he had tried everything he knew to train Topaz, and now, after one conversation, the little dog had finally understood what was required and had started doing it perfectly. But I cautioned Sylvia that it was important to keep up the routine with Topaz, praising him every time he went on the paper.

Things went well until Sylvia went to her summer home in North Carolina. The change in routine and location disturbed Topaz and he started having accidents again.

Sylvia called and I asked her about her new schedule. She told me that in North Carolina she expected Topaz to go outside the house, which had a large garden. This was completely different from what was required of him at home in Manhattan. The confusion had caused the problem we had solved in New York to resurface.

I explained to Sylvia that everything was brand new for Topaz in North Carolina. Fortunately, she had recovered her health and was able to take Topaz outside, but Topaz had not yet made the connection between going outside and relieving himself. Sylvia was frustrated because he often relieved himself inside as soon as he returned from a walk. Of course he did, because that was the routine he was used to.

I told Sylvia to try to connect with Topaz telepathically whenever they went outside, and to send him the physical feelings and urgency of having to go to the bathroom so that he could understand what she wanted. I also communicated with him and explained that as this house had a lovely garden, he could relieve himself outside.

At first we didn't have much success and Sylvia called me back, complaining that she walked Topaz three times a day but he always had an indoor accident right after his walk. When I connected to Topaz, I got a picture of a 'walk' that was very short indeed, perhaps no more than three minutes, and certainly not long enough for a dog who is not sure what to do. Don't forget that dogs like to sniff several dozen spots before deciding where to go, and this can be quite time-consuming even without the added element of Topaz's confusion. I told Sylvia she had to walk Topaz for at least twenty minutes each time, to give him a chance to understand what she wanted and to perform accordingly. I told her to use voice commands, and transmit feelings of urgency telepathically to Topaz, so he would get the idea of relieving himself in the garden before he went back inside the house.

This seemed to do the trick and Topaz soon understood that the change in his location had resulted in a change in what was required of him. He stopped soiling indoors. I cautioned Sylvia there was a slight chance she might undergo another period of difficulty once she changed houses back to Manhattan. It was my feeling, though, that Topaz had the hang of what was expected of him in New York and would not have a problem readjusting to that routine.

Though her business often requires her to be in New York, I wish Sylvia could stay in North Carolina, because Topaz has told me he loves it there. He enjoys the romps in the lovely garden and being able to watch the garden through the windows of the house when he is inside with Sylvia.

The only problem now is that telepathic communication has changed Topaz's whole personality. He has asked me why Sylvia can't talk to him the same way I can. I've told him that she will be able to and that she is working very hard to learn how to do it. Sylvia has told me Topaz now expects to talk; that he literally starts 'talking' whenever she starts speaking and expects to be understood. She can see it in his face. However, much like Sonny, when the topic turns to a problem area, Topaz is not nearly so interested in the conversation.

Larkspur

I had a very sad case with a cat named Larkspur. His owners consulted me because he was having accidents all over the house. At first I thought it was a typical litter box problem, but when I connected telepathically to the cat, I discovered his owners were always leaving him unexpectedly for long periods of time while they travelled. Though they had had Larkspur since he was a kitten, they had never bothered to establish a routine with him, and the poor cat never knew what was going to happen from one day to the next. Just as some parents don't tell their children what is happening even if it impacts on them dramatically, so, too, did Larkspur's owners fail to inform him of the upcoming changes in his environment. Because of this, he lived in a state of distress.

Once, when the couple left the country, Larkspur was sent to live with the man's mother for three months, an arrangement the cat liked because the woman was very kind to him and paid him a lot of attention. During that time, Larkspur didn't have a single accident.

But for the next trip, the couple decided to leave Larkspur with the man's sister for six months. The sister was far less patient with animals than her mother had been, especially after Larkspur started having accidents. She raised her voice to the cat and even struck him. Though I could fully understand her desire to maintain a clean house, free from the smell and stains that accompany pet accidents, I don't agree with her technique. The angrier she got, the more frightened and confused Larkspur became.

Though I tried to explain it to them, Larkspur's owners

couldn't see the connection between their erratic schedule and their cat's accidents. They failed to understand the importance of establishing a good routine to help their cat behave as they wished. Larkspur was unsure of their expectations of him. Because he didn't have one certain place to go to the bathroom, he became confused and started relieving himself wherever he happened to be at the moment.

When I connected to Larkspur telepathically, I discovered there was also an element of anger in his behaviour. His life was a series of scenes – his family packing and leaving him again and again – and it distressed him terribly. The only way he knew to let them know how unhappy he was and that he didn't want them to leave him again was to make a mess in the house.

When I explained this to the owners, they said they had to travel because their business required it. I can certainly understand how, in some lines of work, this may be true. But my immediate thought was, why have a pet if you travel so much that you cannot give it a proper home? Time and again, I find people acquire pets for reasons of their own, giving little or no thought to the needs of the animal.

While I am discussing the importance of establishing a routine with your pet, I would like to take the opportunity to talk about selecting an animal that suits your lifestyle. Never get a pet just because it is cute, or the fashionable animal of the moment. And don't allow your children to pressure you into getting a pet unless it is something *you* truly want, because the responsibility for its care and training will almost certainly fall on you, especially after the novelty of the animal wears off.

Individual breeds have well-documented characteristics. There are several good books which outline the personality traits and care requirements of the various breeds of dog or cat. Some breeds are good with children; some excel as protective companions. Some breeds are lively, while others are quieter. You should do some research and pick a pet whose known habits are compatible with your lifestyle. For example, if you live in a penthouse apartment in a city, you would have trouble meeting the needs of a large dog which requires vigorous daily exercise to maintain its physical health and mental outlook. Nor should you get a pet if you have very little time. They need human companionship to thrive, and it is cruel to keep an animal in isolation. Dogs and cats can be very destructive if they are bored or lonely. Bored dogs chew up furniture and clothing, cats claw furniture and break knick-knacks to amuse themselves when they feel neglected.

Like children, animals need guidance, training and companionship. They require a commitment of time and caring to thrive. Puppies are not born with an innate understanding that they must relieve themselves outside and not on your carpets. You must teach them what you expect, and show them where to go. Cats have a natural inclination to exercise their claws by scratching, and furniture fits that need quite nicely. You must gently teach them that furniture is not to be scratched, and provide them with a suitable alternative. Such training requires patience and compassion.

If you love your furniture more than you love your pet, then don't have a pet.

Again, the easiest way to avoid problems with your pet is to establish a reliable routine in the beginning and stick with it. Don't constantly change the rules or your expectations, because your pet cannot keep up with such inconsistency. Dogs must be walked every day, both for exercise and for the opportunity to relieve themselves. They need play and human companionship. If an animal is to be left alone during the day while you are at work, exercise it before you leave and you will often find that helps to solve problems of boredom and chewing while you are gone. If pets receive sufficient exercise, then they will be tired and settle down far more easily at night.

Proper exercise is necessary to create a happy, contented and well-behaved dog. It also helps maintain your pet's health and increases his life span. You might find that even if you don't particularly enjoy walking alone, walking with your canine companion can be enormous fun, and will probably add several years to your life span as well.

Cats require a clean litter box, and will start soiling if you fail in the routine of cleaning it regularly. If they have a dirty litter box, they will find some clean place to go.

All animals need fresh, nutritious food and clean water daily. Though animals do not require many different flavours of food, they enjoy some variety. They love to have the odd bit of fresh chicken or fish. Most pets will eat almost any nutritious, flavourful food that is served to them, but like humans, they do have their individual dislikes. My Wellington loves tuna, but does not like salmon.

Though some variety in diet is good, you shouldn't

change your pet's diet drastically all the time because it upsets their digestive systems and breaks their routine. They should be fed at the same time each day, and in the same location. Some pets have a favourite dish and will not eat from any other. If this is the case with your pet, respect his feelings. And do be careful the food you buy is not loaded with fillers or chemical preservatives. These contribute to ill health over a period of time.

All animals need open and regular displays of your affection. It is important that they feel a valued part of their human family. They also need to know when their routine is going to change; when you will be gone and for how long; when a new pet is coming in; or when you plan to move. It may sound silly for me to say you must discuss these things with your pet, but taking the time to do so can truly save you much difficulty down the road.

If you do have to alter the routine, remember that all animals are different. If your pets have trouble adapting to the requirements of a new environment, just be patient with them until you can establish a new routine. The establishment of such routines early on with your pet will make for a mutually rewarding and satisfying relationship. Pets want to please us but before they can do so, we have to communicate clearly what we expect of them. Once we get our pets into a good routine, the rest is pure enjoyment.

Sometimes, despite the best care in the world, your pet becomes ill. With the help of my angel guides, I have been able to heal many animals. In the next chapter, I will tell you how this gift was given to me and share some remarkable stories of animals who have regained their health after their owners brought them to me for treatment.

CHAPTER 7

Healing with the angels: when your pet is ill

When a beloved pet becomes ill or is injured, it can turn your world upside-down. Nothing makes a pet owner more desperate than being told their animal companion is terminally ill or mortally injured, and the best thing they can do is to put it out of its misery. Veterinarians save the lives of thousands of sick and injured animals every year, but there is only so much they can do. So, many clients bring an animal to me for healing after it has been injured or diagnosed with a serious illness, and their vets have told them there is no hope of recovery.

I did not come to animal healing lightly. I had to endure much pain and suffering in my own life to prepare me properly for the role I have today, and I had to be trained by my angel guides to use correctly the power they give me to heal the animals that are brought to me.

Of course, I cannot heal all injuries or cure all illness. Sometimes an animal is ready to pass over, and we should not interfere with its decision to go. This can be very difficult for some people who are determined to hang on to their pet at all costs. But often, they do not stop to consider the cost to the animal in terms of pain and suffering.

I always recommend people to continue with regular

veterinary care even though most animals tell me they do not like going to the vet. In that respect they are like many people who don't enjoy going to the doctor or dentist, but sometimes it is necessary and for their own good.

Though I can never promise what the outcome will be, healing always relieves pain. Sometimes there will be a complete recovery; for other animals, their time has come to leave this earth and journey on. In these cases, there is nothing I can do, as all my healing power comes from my guides and its effectiveness varies in each individual case. But even when an animal passes over, I find I am still able to help grieving owners accept their loss, and remember the many hours of joy their pet brought them during its life on this earth.

I never cease to be amazed at the way my angel guides work through me. I am constantly being trained by them so that I may serve as an effective channel for their healing energy, and I have discovered that each guide has a different method of working. My main guide, Dr David Thompson, was a battlefield surgeon during the First World War. He taught me to work with energy and perform psychic operations. My second and newer guide, Harry Edwards, was a famous English healer who died in the 1950s. He healed both animals and people. Harry sends healing energy through me and uses my body to direct healing vibrations to the animals I am working on.

I want to point out that guides do not work through humans without first asking for and being granted permission to do so. I have given my guides permission to work through me, but I never allow my body to be completely taken over because I do not feel comfortable with that.

My guides have told me they must train to work in this dimension, so they will know how to heal through me. Older guides are used to visiting this dimension to work. Newer guides have to adjust to the energy frequencies on earth before they can work efficiently through a human physical body. When they first visit, they cannot stay for long because they tire, and the person they are working through tires also. As they adjust to the energy here, they are able to stay for longer periods of time.

I compare the experience of guides visiting this earthly plane to men landing on the moon. On the moon, our astronauts were in a different atmosphere where they floated around and could not breathe without mechanical assist-ance, because they were not used to living in that dimension. So it is for my guides when they come to this dimension. It is important to remember that they do not have a physical body like we do. Their energy pulsates at a higher frequency than ours, so adjustments are necessary in order for them to be effective in their work here.

I must guard my energy to make sure I don't overwork myself. This is very important when you are doing the work that I do. I am working with both my physical and my energy body when I heal, and would quickly become exhausted if I did not rest.

As I mentioned earlier, I have endured much pain over the years. During the course of my life I have had fourteen operations. After a period of illness, including two major interventions, I was told by my surgeon that I would have to live the remainder of my life as a semi-invalid. After hearing the news, I was determined that in no way was that going to happen to me. I refused to accept the prognosis from my surgeon, and made up my mind that I was never going to have another operation as long as I lived. I did not at that time realize that positive thinking could make me well, and that negative thinking and unhappiness had broken down my immune system and made my body sick.

Through positive thinking and determination, and by not accepting the doctor's sentence of life as a semi-invalid, I began my journey as a healer. I was determined to heal myself. I turned in another direction, away from despair to hope, from resignation to determination. Over the next two years, I steadily climbed back to good health. I was able to mend my body by seeing myself as constantly well. I now look back and feel as if that was another life, but I know it was an essential part of my training, all meant to prepare me for my eventual work as a healer and animal communicator.

Because I have experienced pain and self-healing in my own body, I know what it is like for animals. I put myself into their bodies and feel what they feel, so that it is easier for me to determine what is bothering them. Wherever they hurt, I hurt. Wherever they experience discomfort, I feel the same sensations in the corresponding part of my body. With the help of my guides, I am able to determine exactly what is bothering the animal and whether it can be healed. I do not have to guess.

Now I will tell you about some incredible animals and their owners whom I have been privileged to help within the last few years.

Magic

Mary Lynn Mombray was one of my first clients. One day, she rang me and said her cat, Magic, was ill and would probably have to have surgery. She asked to bring him to me for healing, saying the vet had told her he had heart problems.

She brought the cat to my studio, and I asked Magic for permission to help him feel better by putting my hands on him.

I always get down to the animal's level to connect with their energy so they feel comfortable. Though it takes a few minutes, usually they settle down in a spot underneath the table, on their owner's knee or on the sofa. Then I can work with them. Cats especially hate being taken out of their own environment so it takes them a little longer to relax.

First, I speak to them in a soft voice and tell them how beautiful they are. I then ask for permission to stroke them and make them feel better. Magic was very laid back. As I touched him, I started to feel the healing energy come through into my hands. I asked St Francis to help me. When the energy comes through my hands, I get a tingling feeling and my hands become very warm and turn a golden colour. This change is visible to the naked eye and I have often had clients comment on the colour of my hands as I work to heal their pet.

When I understand what is wrong with the animal, I put my hands on the part of the animal that is affected. I then wait for the lights that I use for healing to come down to me. I was given a beautiful blue light to use on Magic.

I put my hands on the cat and could feel the vibrations

passing through him from the healing and the energy flowing from my guides through my hands. As I transmitted the energy, I felt the cat relaxing. All the animals I heal know that I am trying to help them. They sense this on the telepathic level. I then visualized the blue light going all through the cat's body, cleansing the impurities and blockages from the heart.

I worked on Magic with my guides for about twenty minutes, using blue then gold and finally white lights to heal him. It may take longer than twenty minutes with some animals, but that is about the average length of time the healing energy flows. I work on an animal until the energy doesn't come any more, at which point I realize my guides are finished.

This is just the first step. I also like to have a photograph of each animal I am working with, so, at night, when the universe is still, I can continue to heal them. Some of my most powerful healing is done at night, when I am distant (in the geographical sense only) from the animals my guides and I are actually working upon. Before I go to sleep, I look at each photograph and mentally prepare myself for the night's work. When I picked up Magic's picture, I knew the guides were going to do more healing on the cat that night.

Clients sometimes feel a bit strange about the 'absent healing' I do during the night. It's quite simple really. Normally I am wakened by my guides and go to work again. I use my mind energy and am able to do healing on the sick or injured animal even though my physical body is still asleep. I also converse telepathically with the animals I am healing. I tell them what I am going to do and they understand and are completely willing. I then go back to them and give more of a boost to the healing. The only difference is that I am not actually there; I do it through visualization. And my guides are always working with me, particularly on the animals that are very sick.

Sometimes absent healing goes on for a week, and sometimes it is necessary to get people to bring their animals back in again for hands-on healing. My guides tell me what is necessary for each individual case. They diagnose and decide on a course of treatment, much like any veterinarian would.

Magic required only one more absent healing session. Within a week, he had completely recovered and Mary Lynn reported they had no further problems.

Funa

For five years, Mary Denney had visited one veterinarian after another, trying to find out what was wrong with her cat, Funa. No one could determine what ailed the cat, which suffered from constant digestive disturbances. He'd been ill for so long Mary couldn't remember when he'd been well. He often couldn't keep food in his stomach, vomiting up almost everything he was fed. He was thin and lethargic. Mary was fearful the cat might die soon.

Mary rang me in desperation after hearing me speak about animal communication at a gathering for people interested in metaphysics. She told me about her cat and asked if I could help. This was very soon after the beginning of my training as a healer and I was not sure what I could do, but I agreed to try.

I closed my eyes and asked Dr Thompson if he could help me with the cat. I connected to both Mary's cats through my energy and visualized where they slept at night. I described the scene for Mary who confirmed that what I was seeing was accurate. One of the cats told me he loved to have his head rubbed while the other didn't. Mary confirmed this was true, also.

I started to concentrate on Funa and immediately began to feel ill in my physical body. The sick cat told me he had been ill for a long time and was dying. He was in a state of panic about his illness. I smelled a chemical smell and knew the cat's illness had been caused by swallowing something. The cat sent me a picture of Mary's laundry room and I knew something had happened to Funa there. I felt the cat's illness was due to some sort of chemical exposure and told Mary so. I wondered if it was possible the cat had swallowed some chemical, as I could feel that the lining of his intestines was very sore and raw, which had resulted in the chronic digestive upsets.

'Has Funa by any chance licked up some bleach?' I asked Mary.

Mary became excited, telling me that five years before, the cat had fallen into a washing machine full of bleach, but she hadn't realized at the time that he had swallowed any of the caustic poison. I realized the bleach had caused extensive damage to the cat's stomach and intestinal lining and that damage was what had made him chronically ill for the past five years.

I then called on my guides to help me heal the cat. Dr Thompson came forward to assist me and instructed and guided me in the healing operation. I visualized a laser beam cutting the cat open and lights were given to me to work with. As each light was handed to me, I was told what to do. After the cat was opened up, I could actually see his ulcerated stomach, and I knew how desperately sick the animal truly was. I saw a beautiful golden light and knew it was meant to help me heal the cat. I visualized the light healing and repairing the cat's stomach lining. I pushed energy through the cat's intestines with the golden light, pushing out all the sickness.

After the gold, I was given a beautiful blue light, and told to visualize this going all through the intestines, soothing and healing the damage. I used the laser beam to suture the cat closed, and bathed his entire body with another beautiful light, violet blue this time, and left the cat in that light to protect him as he continued to heal. Mary reported that the cat had fallen into a deep sleep during the course of the operation. I myself felt exhausted as the work of healing the cat drained all my energy.

That night, my guides wakened me at 3 a.m. and I knew my work with Funa was not finished. I felt my energy body joining with the universal energy stream on the astral plane. I visualized my astral hands and my mind energy healing the body of the sick cat while he slept. I was very aware of my guides working with me.

Mary reported the cat was visibly recovered the next day, with a much improved appetite. For the next two weeks, my guides and I continued to do healing on Funa every night. Mary reported that the cat had made a complete recovery. He was gaining weight and had a normal appetite once again.

Mr Clinker

I had become a regular guest on the Scott Cluthe radio show in Houston. Each time I was on, the phone bank lit up with calls from pet owners anxious to recover a lost pet, or to solve some behavioural or health problem. I soon found I was quickly able to connect with the animals in question through the owner's energy. I often talked to the animals live on the air, telling the owners things only they would know about their animals, such as having an operation or illness, or the fact that this was not the animal's first home or that their previous owner was cruel to them. The astounded owners always confirmed as accurate whatever I relayed to them from their pets, though they couldn't begin to understand how I knew what I knew.

A man named Irwin called one day, very distressed about his cat, Mr Clinker, who had been diagnosed with terminal feline leukaemia. Mr Clinker had a large tumour on his jaw. The vet said the tumour could be removed, but because of its size and location, the lower jaw would be lost. Irwin declined the disfiguring surgery, unwilling to put his beloved pet through so much suffering. In his own words, he instituted a 'death watch'.

Daily, the tumour grew in size, causing Mr Clinker terrible pain. He snored and experienced bouts of apnea that meant he had trouble breathing. His appetite faded to nothing. One day, quite by chance, Irwin tuned in to the Scott Cluthe show and caught the very end of the programme. He called immediately, and I spoke to him after the broadcast ended. Despite Houston's vastness, Irwin happened to live within walking distance of my home, which was fortunate as he could not drive because of poor vision. I went to see Mr Clinker at Irwin's home.

When I arrived, I was astounded to see a garden full of art, including a lovely bronze figure. Irwin turned out to be the proverbial starving artist, a man who had very little money but a heart full of love and compassion for animals. He had taken in eight cats whom he fed and doted upon.

I was alarmed when I saw the size of the tumour on Mr Clinker's jaw. When I connected with the cat, I realized he was still a bit wild. Because he was so very sick, Irwin had put him into his own room where the other cats could not disturb him. I felt Mr Clinker's energy and waited for the cat to accept my presence. It took him a little while, and I realized the cat was prone to hiss and spit. I asked the cat if I could help him and told him I would be very honoured if he allowed me to do so. Mr Clinker thought about it for a while, then replied that he would allow me to help. Again, I felt the wonderful warm energy coming into my hands and knew healing power was already being transmitted.

I put my hands on Mr Clinker and he offered no resistance. I felt in my own throat how sore the cat's throat was. I felt the blood disorder, which Irwin later identified as leukaemia. I could see a beautiful green light coming down and knew this was the one I would use to heal the cat. I took the green light from the eyes down through the neck and the rest of Mr Clinker's body, and while drawing it through I could feel the vibrations within the cat's body and knew healing was taking place. I imagined the impurities all being taken away and his blood becoming healthy and well. I talked to him and told him he too must imagine this, seeing himself whole and healthy.

I then started healing the cat's throat and jaw. I was again given a beautiful healing light, this time royal blue, which I visualized on his throat. At the same time, healing energy was being passed through my hands.

Mr Clinker was feeling very relaxed. The healing continued for some twenty minutes, then I felt the energy withdraw from my hands and knew the healing had been completed for that session. I thanked Mr Clinker and told Irwin I would be doing more healing at night. Mr Clinker also required several more hands-on healing sessions. I asked Irwin to keep me informed of the cat's progress.

Irwin was delighted with the results as Mr Clinker seemed to be recovering well after three days. Then he took Mr Clinker to his regular vet the next week, and other than a little ulceration secondary to a minor throat inflammation, there was absolutely no indication of the large tumour that just the week before had threatened to end the cat's life. Mr Clinker was fully and completely cured.

Mr Clinker lived another eleven months after my guides healed him, free of pain and without obvious signs of illness. He had a healthy appetite and renewed vigour for life. Then one night he passed to the other side in his sleep, having reached the ripe old cat age of seventeen.

Jean Lafitte

My co-author Pat's son Carter had been greatly disappointed to discover he couldn't fit out his new pirate turtle with a brass earring and peg-leg, but nonetheless Jean Lafitte had turned out to be a most satisfactory pet. Pat's family had owned the turtle for almost two years, and in that time his shell had grown from less than two inches to more than six inches across.

During the first cold snap of 1993, Jean Lafitte stopped eating. This was puzzling because he'd always had quite an appetite. Pat phoned the vet and he told her that when turtles get cold, they often go off their food. He advised her to move the aquarium away from the window, where it might be draughty, to a more sheltered spot inside the house. She moved it to her dining room which has no exterior windows.

But the move didn't help. Jean Lafitte still wouldn't eat. Within a few days, he started to drift aimlessly in his tank, spewing mucus from both nostrils. Pat's son was terribly upset and she felt panicky, wondering what to do to restore the turtle to good health. It had now been seven days since he had eaten anything.

That morning, I'd made arrangements to meet Pat to work on our etiquette book, but she was distracted and worried about the turtle, so she couldn't concentrate.

I immediately picked up on Pat's distress. When she explained, I offered to speak to the turtle and find out what was wrong, an offer which astounded her. Pat had no idea what I was talking about. Though we had been friends for more than a year, I had never mentioned my ability to communicate with animals to her.

Briefly, I described my telepathic gift. Though Pat was quite sceptical, she felt so desperate she would have tried anything to save the turtle.

I asked Pat for the turtle's name. When she told me,

'Jean Lafitte,' I couldn't help but reply, 'That's quite a posh name for a turtle.'

'He's quite a posh turtle,' Pat responded, still not sure of the value of this experiment.

I closed my eyes and within moments, I was able to tell Pat that the turtle was unhappy about his tank being moved from its accustomed spot in her son's bedroom window. He wanted it moved back immediately. Pat was amazed because she had only just moved the tank a few days before and hadn't mentioned it to me.

The turtle told me he was dying. He told me he was very sad because he loved Pat's family and did not want to leave them. Then he started to give me a laundry list of the things that were wrong in his habitat, all things that had contributed, along with the cold weather, to his illness.

Speaking in a small, tinny voice, he told me he had outgrown his aquarium, and that it didn't have any stones on the bottom where he could get proper traction to walk and dive. He sent me a picture of his feet slipping on the bottom of the tank. He also informed me his water needed to be much deeper so he could swim, and filtrated to stay fresher and cleaner. 'As long as I was a small turtle, this tank was fine, but now I am too big for it and have no room to swim and the water gets dirty too quickly,' the turtle told me. Finally, Jean Lafitte asked for a larger rock for basking and diving, a green plant and a small fish for a companion.

Pat quickly drove to the nearest pet store, abandoning the book project to rescue the turtle, though she was still unconvinced of the wisdom of what she was doing. I have quite a sense of humour and I think Pat wondered if she hadn't become the unwitting victim of an elaborate prank. To encourage her as she left, I emphasized again that speed was necessary as the turtle was near death.

While Pat was in the store, she made the mistake of telling the owner she was buying the goldfish for her turtle. He looked at her as if she was crazy and told her, 'Lady, you can't put a goldfish into a tank with a turtle. He'll eat it.'

'Oh, no,' Pat assured him. 'My turtle told me he just wants the fish for a friend.'

'Your turtle told you what?' the man said, looking at Pat even more strangely.

Pat turned her head as if she hadn't heard him and hurried out of the store with her $79.53 worth of turtle goods, thinking it was all an act of futility, that it was too late and the turtle was going to die anyway, and she'd be stuck with an elaborate turtle habitat and no bread or milk for the rest of the week.

Pat set up the new aquarium in her son's bedroom window and moved the turtle into his new home. For the next three days, she hovered over Jean Lafitte, watching closely for some sign of improvement. There was none, but at least he didn't get any sicker; he was still alive.

On the fourth day, the turtle ate two sticks of turtle food and Pat noticed his nose was no longer running. She and her children celebrated this obvious turn for the better and called to inform me of the good news.

Jean Lafitte continued to improve. By the seventh day, he was swan-diving off his new basking rock, and marching around his tank like some lord of the deep, fully recovered. Pat called and thanked me profusely, still not quite sure what she was thanking me for, but knowing that somehow

My grandmother, Emmaline Robishaw, who first
taught me respect for nature.

Modelling days. I used to wear fur until I realised how many animals had suffered for me simply to be able to wear a jacket.

Stacey with Hubert, who learned not to play with the mini blinds at midnight.

Gayle with Sonny, a stallion who is learning to be more co-operative.
(*Patricia B. Smith*)

Karen with Zuki, whom I healed after he became ill due to another iguana's intense jealousy.
(*Patricia B. Smith*)

With Bella, my beloved Rhodesian Ridgeback, about
four months before she passed over.
(*Patricia B. Smith*)

Foxy who – with Wellington and Honey – brings me great comfort.
(*Patricia B. Smith*)

I was at least partly responsible for saving the turtle's life. She didn't understand it but, to her credit, she accepted it. That was Pat's introduction to the world of animal communication.

Unfortunately, the goldfish had become a bit more relaxed too, losing that look of sheer terror he'd assumed when he first realized he was confined in a ten-gallon tank with a turtle. One evening when Pat came home, she went to greet Jean Lafitte and noticed there was no goldfish in the tank. She looked everywhere, but there weren't that many places for a goldfish to hide. In a panic, she called me and I immediately connected to Jean Lafitte, asking him where the goldfish was.

'I've eaten him,' he replied. 'I knew I would never get the fish if I'd told you I was going to eat him.'

I chastised him for misrepresenting the real reason he wanted the fish. To this day, I haven't forgiven myself for my role in the hapless goldfish's death. He deceived me, that turtle. I didn't realize he was so crafty. He told me he wanted a friend, when all he really wanted was a snack!

For her part, Pat thinks that perhaps there were some nutrients, minerals or vitamins in that fish that Jean Lafitte needed to complete his recovery. At any rate, she hasn't given him any more fish to munch upon, and he continues to be a happy, healthy turtle. As often happens with animals I help, Jean Lafitte has turned into a regular gossip and now keeps me informed of all the goings on in Pat's house, especially noticing when she fails to wash up the dishes. Pat just wishes he would stop telling me when she hasn't done the laundry.

Beau

My friend, Donna, brought her dog, Beau, in to me for healing. She had taken him to the vet because he was limping, but the vet said Beau's problems were the result of his advanced age and he could do nothing to help him. When I connected to Beau's energy, I picked up all five of Donna's pets. A cat named Spankie came forward and informed me that Beau suffered terribly with the pain in his feet and legs, but tried to hide his pain because he didn't want to worry his family.

I asked Donna about the dog's health, and she said she worried because Beau sometimes had real difficulty getting going in the morning.

Spankie was clamouring to be heard again. 'Beau's feet do hurt him. He does not want Mummy to know, but I am the biggest kitty and when I speak, no one talks back to me. Beau has taken care of all of us for a long time, so now I am going to take care of Beau by telling his secret.'

I told Donna what the cat had said, that the dog suffered with his feet but kept his pain hidden because he didn't want to worry her. With Donna's permission, I started healing the dog, who quickly regained his former boisterous and active nature. The quietness and inactivity Donna had put down to the onset of old age was actually due to the pain from Beau's congenital foot problem. Once my guides relieved the dog's pain, he became his old self again.

There is an interesting 'foot' note to this story. Donna brought Beau in several more times for healing, along with his brother Cody who had an ear problem. I noticed both dogs had skin rashes, which Donna said their vet had not been able to clear up. I asked my guides for help and they told me that both dogs were allergic to the wheat in their food. I advised Donna to switch to a diet of rice and fish for her dogs and the skin rash disappeared within a matter of weeks.

Beau has since died of old age, but it gave Donna great comfort to see the relief from pain my guides were able to give him, making his last few months comfortable and productive.

Heidi

Over the Christmas holidays of 1995, my dear friend Valerie Patrick called me in a panic about her beautiful German Shepherd, Heidi. She'd been having some health problems and the vet who examined her found she had a tumour on the right side of her back. The doctor wanted to do a biopsy, but Val didn't consent to the procedure because the previous summer Heidi had suffered two mild heart attacks following anaesthesia for a constriction in her throat. The anaesthesia was too strong and it weakened Heidi's heart.

Heidi managed for a while, but it was obvious she didn't have her usual strength and vigour. Finally, Val called me in distress at two o'clock in the morning. Heidi had suffered a third heart attack, much more serious this time. I went and laid my hands on Heidi, and sent healing energy coursing through her body. She recovered but she was still very weak, so I continued to work on her.

By then the growth on Heidi's back was about the size of a walnut and quite prominent, with hairs sticking out around it. Val said everyone who came to visit noticed it. Val knew she was going to have to do something about the tumour, but she hated to take Heidi in for another operation because of what had happened the last time.

I started directing healing energy through the tumour, visualizing it shrinking in size and being absorbed harmlessly into Heidi's body. I worked on her with absent healing every night for several weeks. Six weeks later, Val looked for the tumour, but it was gone. Val called Ruby, her maid, and asked her which side was Heidi's tumour on. Ruby looked at Heidi and said, 'It's gone!' There was no trace of the tumour to be found.

A week later, Heidi was scheduled for her regular dental check-up. The vet looked for the tumour and found it wasn't there. Looking for the scar and stitches, he asked Val which vet had performed the surgery. Val didn't know if he was a believer but decided to tell him she had had the surgery done psychically. Predictably, the vet thought she was crazy.

'Are you sure you didn't go to another doctor to have it removed?' the vet asked her.

Val is very spiritual and we've been friends for twenty-one years, but she says sometimes she still can't believe it herself that healing energy from my guides restored Heidi to good health without veterinary intervention.

Normally, as I have stated earlier, I recommend working with vets and continuing regular veterinary care as well as using healing energy. But in this case, Heidi had shown a marked sensitivity to anaesthesia, and I knew a surgical procedure would do her more harm than good, perhaps even kill her. I am thankful I was able to use the healing energy of my guides to heal my friend's dog.

Bravo

A family called me in great distress. Their beloved cat Bravo was ill, but they did not specify the illness to me. They were sceptical of my ability to help their cat, but consulted me, as many clients do, out of desperation.

When they arrived, I placed my hands on the cat and knew he was full of worms, but oddly, not worms common to cats. Bravo's owners confirmed he had worms as they had just come from the vet, who was not able to do anything for the cat because the case was too far advanced.

I asked Bravo if he had eaten anything unusual, and he sent me a picture of a dead possum, so I knew the source of the worm infestation. I also knew the cat was very ill. The worms had formed a sort of ball which was causing a life-threatening intestinal blockage.

Working with my guides, we removed the worms and cured Bravo completely. His owners were thrilled to have their cat restored to good health.

People often ask me when I say I remove something, if I actually see what is being removed. Usually I don't, because the tumour or damaged area is being cleansed with healing lights provided to me by my guides. The healing energy is directed through my hands, which feel tingly and warm while this is happening. At times, the energy flow put through to heal an animal will be so strong it causes my hands to vibrate.

So when I say I remove worms, I don't actually see them. I know only that my guides have removed worms that have been diagnosed by a vet, and that when the cat is taken back for a check-up, the worms are no longer there. The one exception I can remember is the intestinal blockage I discovered in Zuki, the iguana (from Chapter 5).

Crystal

One of my favourite stories of healing concerns a cat brought to me by my client Beverly, who rescues cats. At any given time, Beverly has fifty or more cats in her care and I often help her by collecting food, towels and blankets from my clients.

This cat, which Beverly called Crystal, had no fur whatsoever, and its entire body was covered with open, weeping sores. The vet diagnosed her as having a virus which he said she caught from her mother. He recommended putting the animal out of its misery.

When I connected to the cat, I realized she was in extreme pain. I asked, as I always do, for her permission to begin healing, and the cat agreed, requesting only that I did not touch her. I reassured Crystal I would not put my hands on her. Her wounds looked so dreadful I would have been afraid to do so for fear of causing her even more pain.

I started to heal the cat through its aura, sending healing light through by holding my hands about two inches away from her body. I healed Crystal with absent healing every night for a week, and then Beverly returned with the cat to my studio. At first, I thought the cat hadn't made much progress, then I felt a surge of strength go through my body and realized she had grown stronger. I was encouraged. It was given to me to tell Beverly to start putting antiseptic ointment on the sores and feed the cat a diet of plain boiled rice and fish.

When Beverly returned the following week, it was obvious Crystal was feeling much better. The sores were healing and there were tufts of fur starting to grow in patches. I saw Crystal once more, then continued absent healing for several weeks. Now Crystal is completely healthy. Her sores are all healed and she has a full coat of beautiful beige fur and is ready to be placed in an adoptive home.

A lost pet is just as upsetting for pet owners as having a sick pet. In some ways, it is even more distressing, because you are never quite sure what has happened to your pet if you can't find it. In the next chapter, I will share some stories of lost pets, and give pointers for the best course to follow if your pet should stray.

CHAPTER 8

Wanderlust: adventures we could do without

When a pet is lost, it can be devastating to a family. The frantic neighbourhood search, the posters tacked to street lights, the walking and calling your pet's name in vain, can fray even the steadiest nerves.

The first thing I do is calm the owners and get them to give me as much information as possible about the lost pet. While they are talking, they usually focus and settle down sufficiently for me to connect to their lost pet through their energy.

Happily, in the majority of cases I pick the animal right up. The ones who are truly lost are always confused and frightened, and eager to find their way back home. On the other hand, the ones who have left home by choice will not even consider going back, particularly cats, which are far less tolerant of ill treatment from their humans than dogs are. At the very least, I can gather enough information from the lost animal for its owners to launch a targeted search. In some cases, we will be lucky and find the animal, but sadly, I cannot find all lost animals. I can only do so much. The owner is the one who has to go out and put

up posters in the target area and find the landmarks I give
them from pictures the animals send me.

The joy I feel when I succeed in recovering an animal is
incredible because I know the odds can be long against the
animal ever being found. Prayer, good luck, and the ability
of the missing animal to communicate with pictures and
feelings are my strongest allies in the search. Some animals
communicate more clearly than others, and that is always a
big help.

We've all read stories of incredible journeys undertaken
by lost pets trying to find their families. Some such journeys
can cover hundreds of miles. We even hear of animals
tracking their families across country.

A very famous case more than twenty years ago involved
a family which moved from New York to California, leaving
their year-old black and white cat in the care of a neigh-
bouring family until they could get settled in their new
home and send for him. The cat had an unusual marking
on his stomach which appeared to be a perfect outline of
the continental United States. Unfortunately, he ran away
within a few days of the move, and the neighbours called
their friends in California to tell them of the disappearance.

Thirteen months later, across more than 3,000 miles of
rugged terrain, through all kinds of weather and dangers, a
scraggly black and white cat with what appeared to be
a map of the United States on its stomach showed up at
the family's back door in California, miaowing to be let in.
This heroic feat catapulted the feline to brief fame, with
his picture appearing in newspapers all over the country.

But how did this remarkable cat find his family? How
did he know where to go when he had never even seen

their new home or had no idea exactly where they were moving? The answer is that he tracked their energy. The bond between the cat and his family was so strong he was literally able to use their energy as a lifeline during the long months he was separated from them.

People always want to know: how do lost animals find their way home? Why is it that some succeed in their quest and others do not?

There's quite a bit of science involved in the answers to these questions, which I will try to explain clearly so that you may understand how the homing instinct works in animals.

You already know we are all surrounded by energy. Energy in its purest form is the life force of the universe. It flows around us and through us. In fact, our bodies are energy arranged in solid form. In the popular science fiction film *Star Wars*, this energy was called 'the force', and I must say George Lucas's concept of how energy fields work is not far off the mark.

You also know that animals communicate telepathically, using their mind energy to transmit back and forth pictures, thoughts and feelings. We do this also, though unknowingly, and it is this constant stream of mind energy we put out through the electromagnetic fields of the earth which our pets may use to track their way back to us. Even though your animal is lost, he can still pick up the thoughts and feelings transmitting out through your energy. The energy link is not broken even though the physical link may well be.

Like humans, animals have varying degrees of intelligence and sensitivity. Some humans can cook or draw or play the

piano, while many others can't do any of these things. So
it is with animals. Some can tune in quite easily to their
owners' thoughts and feelings; others are not as adept.

Sometimes an animal's willingness to communicate
depends upon the motivation of the moment. If your pet
has left home because he is angry or jealous of a new
arrival, he may not be nearly as anxious to be reunited with
you as you are with him. Other animals are overcome by
fear and decide it is safer to stay in their new location than
risk the dangers of an attempted journey home, while others
are confident enough to trust all their senses and tune in
to the energy fields where they will be able to pick up the
mind energy you are constantly transmitting.

Remember, you already have an energy link with your
pet because you have lived together and established a pattern
of communication. That energy link is just like a radio
wave. You can tune your energy in to that of your pet as
if you were tuning in to a radio station. Each time you
think of your pet, he is on the receiving end of the thought,
almost as if you were calling him on the telephone. The
only difference is that you are probably not attuned to the
energy line like your pet is, so you don't 'hear' him when
he communicates with you.

If an animal is trying to reunite with its family, it will
instinctively tune in to vibrations in the universal energy
fields. Some animals have a heightened awareness of their
senses which functions like a built-in compass, and they
can feel the pull of a particular direction when they tune
in to your energy. Other animals do not have this ability,
and when I tune in to them I can feel their confusion and
fear. A fearful, confused animal is much more difficult to

recover than a brave and confident one, because the fearful animal will not take the necessary steps to find its way home. The truth is, only a small percentage of lost animals ever find their way home.

Many times, particularly in the case of valuable animals, a pet hasn't been lost; it's been stolen, and you can be sure those responsible for the theft will do everything in their power to make sure they aren't discovered. I have the best chance of finding an animal which has truly been lost, who can provide me with good information in the form of images and feelings about their journey from home, which I can then reconstruct to send the owners on a targeted search for their pet. Some will remember more clearly the route they have taken while others will be confused. If they are confused, that confusion is all they can send me, so it becomes very difficult for me to get any information about their location.

If I am lucky, the animal will be able to send me a picture of a distinctive landmark. I had a client whose cat, Jaspar, was able to send me an image of a church with a dark green roof that he said was nearby. Though the church was more than ten miles away, the owner was able to retrieve his cat because the location and identity of that particular building were unmistakable.

Sometimes, when a cat has been chasing a bird or a dog has been chasing a squirrel, they are so preoccupied that they lose track of their surroundings. When they realize they are in unfamiliar territory, they become disoriented and panicky. These cases are difficult to resolve also, because during the chase the animal will have paid no attention to its route, only to its prey, so it cannot give me many landmarks or clues to its location.

Workmen visiting your home present another danger. They often leave their vehicles open while they are working, and cats cannot seem to resist investigating an open door. I had a client whose cat hitched a ride in a carpet-cleaning van. When the workers opened the back of their van at their office in the next town, fourteen miles from the woman's home, a cat jumped out. The workmen thought nothing of it until the woman called the next day to ask if they had seen her cat. Though she put up posters near their office, she got no response and presumed her cat was lost for ever. Then, eight weeks later, he showed up at her door, a bit thin but in perfect health.

Some animals get lost when they have been frightened by another animal. A cat who has been chased for several blocks by a large dog is not only confused but terrified, and in mortal fear for its life. In these cases, when I connect to their energy I tell them to stay right where they are, calm themselves and gather their energy. Then I tell them to wait until the universe is still and dark (night), when I will waken and tune in to their energy. I reassure them and tell them to trust their instincts. I reinforce the idea that they are a very smart dog or cat who can easily find their way home under the cover of darkness.

I tune in to them with my ears, so they receive the idea that they must use their ears to check for any noise before they cross a street. If there is noise (a car approaching) I tell them they must be very still and wait for it to be quiet again before crossing. I send the message telepathically with my mind, but also with my body, so the animal knows what he must do to travel safely.

Sometimes they find the courage to start their journey home. It may take a few days or even a few weeks, but usually I can get some of these animals home. A lot depends on the animal's personality, whether it is brave and not over-anxious. If the journey home seems too daunting, they will often stay in their new location and find themselves loving homes.

Many animals become lost because their owner assumes they will be safe no matter what. You should never let your dog or cat roam freely; not only might they get lost, they could also be hit by a car, stolen or attacked by another animal. It is your responsibility as a pet owner to see to the safety and security of your animal. If your dog has proved himself capable of jumping over a high fence or digging underneath it to escape your garden, you must make whatever changes are necessary to provide him with a secure place. Try to send him pictures of the dangers that await in the world outside his fence. If dogs and cats only knew how dangerous the world can be, most of them would never leave their homes. But like children, animals are filled with a sense of adventure that all too often is not accompanied by sufficient caution.

Dogs need walking every day. They need to get out and exercise regularly. Don't feel that just because you have a big garden that is sufficient. Animals are curious, and need to see and understand the world around them. Walking also orients them within their neighbourhood so that it becomes familiar and not as frightening.

Be especially vigilant about your pet's safety when you

go on holiday. If you choose to leave your animal behind, I recommend you hire a knowledgeable pet sitter rather than rely on your neighbours to care for your pet. A few years ago, hardly anyone had heard of a pet sitter, but now they are becoming more popular as people are beginning to realize that being left in a kennel can be a very unhappy experience for an animal. Not only must they endure the stress of all the other cooped-up, frightened and lonely animals barking and yowling, they may also be exposed to contagious diseases or pick up fleas in such an atmosphere.

Animals that have been put in a kennel have no idea why they are there. They don't know if it is a punishment, or if they are to be left there indefinitely. It's like us going to prison. Suddenly, from a comfortable bed and a large garden, they find themselves sleeping on damp concrete and confined to a cage that barely has enough room for them to turn around in. I have treated many behaviour problems in animals that cropped up after the pet was left in a kennel for a week or so.

So, take the time to locate and interview a reliable pet sitter. Ask for references, just as you would if you were leaving your children with someone new. Tell the sitter about your pet's routine, and stress the importance of maintaining that routine. Be sure to explain to your animal that you will be leaving for just a little while, but that someone very nice will come and look after them while you are gone. It is a great comfort to animals when their owners take the time to tell them what is going to happen. That way, they do not get so nervous and confused.

✿

Moving is a very dangerous time for cat owners, as cats have a tendency to form an energy link with their physical location (i.e., your old house). Domestic felines can use that energy link with something scientists call 'psi tracking' to find their way back to their original home, even if it is thousands of miles away. Though scientists have a name for this ability, they don't understand how it works or why cats are equipped with this particular skill.

Remember to confine your cat to one room of your new home for at least a week after you move. The week of confinement allows cats time to form an energy link with their new location, so that when you let them out into the rest of the house, they should be content to stay and not try to roam or run back to their old house.

I have many clients who ask me why all the stray cats in the world arrive on their doorstep. It isn't by accident. It's because they are cat lovers and cats looking for a new home will track positive energy vibrations to a house where they know a cat lover is in residence. Just as a radio wave is picked up by a receiver tuned to the proper channel, cats tune in to the energy vibrations of a cat lover to locate your house, knowing full well they will be welcomed, however reluctantly. They also know, from reading your energy vibrations, that if they stick around long enough they will be regularly fed and well cared for.

*

Technology has brought us a new way to track and recover lost or stolen pets. It is a tiny microchip, first developed to provide irrefutable proof of identity for expensive horses and exotic birds, but it wasn't long before the veterinary community caught on to the usefulness of the idea for their own clientele. The microchip is programmed with a unique identifying code and then injected into your pet with a special hypodermic needle. The newer and more expensive devices can actually be used to track an animal on a geographic map, just like something you would see in a spy movie. The older ones simply provide proof of identity for a recovered animal.

The problem is that there is currently no universal system for identification. Your local animal shelter may subscribe to one of these programmes, but not another. Still, if you allow your pet to roam freely, it might be a good idea to invest in a tracking device. But remember, no device can do the job you as a pet owner must do, which is to provide your animal with a loving, safe and secure environment, so be vigilant in the care of your pet.

In the United States, animal welfare workers believe strongly in county registration programmes in which an ordinance requires you to register your pet for a nominal one-off fee. You are then given a tag to put on your pet's collar. If your pet happens to get lost, the information on the tag will give animal welfare workers all they need to reunite your pet with your family. In counties where these registration programmes are in force, there is a much higher rate of animals being returned to their owners.

In the UK, the Kennel Club, RSPCA and Scottish SPCA have developed PetLog as a national identification scheme. The PetLog collar tag carries a 24-hour helpline number and a unique identification number for your pet. These are logged into a national database, which is used as a reference source for local authorities, the police, and established welfare and rescue organizations. To register, write to PetLog, PO Box 2037, Clarges Street, London W1A 1GP, or call 0171 629 3267/6707. There is a nominal annual fee for the service.

You should ask your vet for details about how to get your pet microchipped. In the UK, this will register you on PetLog automatically.

Now I will share some stories of lost pets and their owners, and how we recovered them and reunited them with their families.

Sugar

Carol Moore has a beloved Maltese dog named Sugar. One day, someone accidentally left the garden gate ajar and Sugar got out. Carol was frantic with worry because she lives close to a major thoroughfare and was afraid Sugar might get hit by a car.

Carol had heard about me through a friend, so she phoned immediately to tell me of Sugar's disappearance. While I was looking at a picture of Sugar, the dog began to communicate with me, relating details of Carol's life that only Sugar, but certainly not I, could know. Carol was overwhelmed with relief, knowing that her dog was well and communicating with me.

Sugar told me her journey began after she left Carol's garden. I was able to pick up Carol's house and garden in great detail. I saw the gate ajar and also told Carol I saw a main road opposite the house to the right. Then Sugar started to tell me about her journey.

First, she crossed the road, being careful to avoid the cars. She told me a woman in a cream-coloured car then picked her up and put her into her car. Next, she complained because her 'mummy', as she referred to Carol, always had a nice, soft towel folded on the car seat for her to rest upon, and there was no towel in this woman's car. She transmitted to my body a feeling of unsteadiness, particularly in my arms and legs, and I knew she'd had difficulty staying on the car seat because the woman's upholstery was slippery. When I told Carol about the towel, she became very excited because she did keep a towel on the car seat for Sugar.

Sugar said they had passed a church on the way, and transmitted a picture of the church to me. She also sent a picture of a supermarket on the left side of the road. Then she transmitted a feeling with her body of the car turning to the left shortly after the supermarket.

Somewhere after the left turn, Sugar sensed the car turning right, and then it pulled into a garage and stopped. She sent this information to me telepathically.

I did not feel any hunger or thirst in Sugar's body, so I knew the people who had picked her up were keeping her well fed and watered. Sugar then told me she was inside a house and flashed me a picture of the home's interior, a cream room with a fireplace. It comforted Carol a lot to know her beloved dog was being looked after, and that she was safe.

A man in the house kept saying to the lady who had

picked Sugar up, 'Let's take the dog back. We have her name on her collar and her owner's address. Let's take her back.' But the woman and children who had picked Sugar up wanted to keep her because she was so pretty. Sugar kept sending me images of the home's interior. Sugar was afraid she might not see Carol again, because the man kept repeating, 'Give the dog back,' and the woman kept answering, 'No.'

I told Carol the only way to get Sugar back was to start praying that the family who had the dog would open their hearts and give her back. I told Carol to put up posters with Sugar's picture and an offer of a reward in the area near the family's house, so Carol recreated Sugar's journey in her car and found the church and the supermarket, just as her pet had described.

Carol had posters made and put them up as I suggested. Late in the afternoon of that same day, Carol received a phone call from a little girl who said they had bought a dog from someone, and this dog had an ID tag. The girl asked if Carol owned a white dog named Sugar, but before Carol could answer, the phone went dead.

Carol was hysterical and thought, 'How could they do that to me?' But as I had suggested, she calmed herself, focused and prayed for her dog's speedy return. I had also told her to have all her friends pray for Sugar's return. Prayer is very powerful, particularly when your pet is lost. The more friends you have praying for your pet's return, the better.

Twenty minutes after the phone call, Carol's doorbell rang and there stood a little girl with Sugar. Carol was overjoyed as she took her dog into her arms. She looked outside and saw the girl's father, who was in a cream-coloured car. Carol was amazed when she saw the car just as I had described it, and vowed to be more careful about making sure that the gate was securely fastened before she let Sugar into the garden unattended.

Madonna

One day I had an unusual phone call from a woman by the name of Salise Shuttlesworth, requesting my help in finding a family of pigs. A former lawyer who had given up her practice to devote herself to the care of orphaned and abandoned animals, Salise is executive director of a no-kill animal shelter in Houston called Special Pals. Their policy is never to put a healthy animal down. The family of pigs had been stolen from this shelter. Although the theft had been on television and in the newspapers, and Salise had issued numerous appeals for the return of her beloved animals, no one responded. My daughter Emma set up an appointment with Salise, who came in right away armed with pictures of her pigs.

When I attempted to establish a telepathic connection with the animals, I was particularly drawn to the energy of the mother pig, Madonna. I couldn't establish a clear link with the piglets, but this did not surprise me. Just as it takes a while for human infants to learn how to talk, infant animals must learn how to communicate telepathically.

As I tuned in to Madonna's energy, I felt a great sadness. I asked her why she was unhappy and she told me one of her babies had died at birth because she had accidentally stepped on it. It made her very sad. She was frightened for her babies and was concerned for their welfare, and for herself and the piglets' father, Dick.

I told Salise first to inform the slaughterhouses about the pigs but she had already done this. She was amazed when I told her about the baby pig that had died at birth. She knew then that I was truly in touch with her pets.

I asked Madonna what she could tell me about the night she and her family had been taken. She sent me a picture of two men who had come in a lorry. She transmitted the colour black, so I knew it was the middle of the night and not the early morning when the pigs were stolen. I got the feeling Madonna knew one of the men who had taken them. Then she told me one of the two had once worked for Salise.

When I told Salise this and gave her the description of the man Madonna had given me, Salise knew exactly who it was. She'd had to dismiss the man a week before, and knew he was likely to hold a grudge and try to get back at Salise by hurting her beloved animals. It is sad when human vindictiveness hurts animals.

I was very impressed with Madonna's intelligence. Her pictures were clear and her telepathic communication was detailed. She left nothing out. She told me two other adult pigs had been taken, which Salise confirmed. Madonna said the two pigs had squealed loudly and been very difficult for the men to catch.

The lorry was backed up to the pen. After the men ushered the squealing pigs into the lorry, Madonna said the door had closed. She could see nothing but sent me with her body telepathically that they had turned to the

right after going down the drive, and then to the left. I felt
the swing in my body when the truck was going around the
turns. Then they went left again. Then Madonna felt she
was on a much busier road because she heard traffic.

I asked Madonna if she had gone a short way or a long
way. She felt it was a long way along a busy road with
many other cars. I felt they must have gone on a major
road because that's the only place there would have been
traffic at that time of night. By indicating with her body
movement, Madonna told me they then took another left
turn. She communicated with me through feelings and her
body senses. I asked her if she could send me any pictures
of where she was, but she was shut up in the dark, so there
were no landmarks to guide our search.

I got an unpleasant feeling in my mouth, and knew
Madonna didn't like the food she was being given. She told
me they had given her some bread and that was all, so I
knew she was hungry. Madonna was concerned about what
was going to happen to her and her babies.

At the time, I asked Salise not to release any of these
details Madonna had given me to the press, because I was
worried there would be a backlash against the sanctuary.
People can sometimes be funny about the work I do. Salise
had already paid a dear price with the loss of her pigs, and
I didn't want anything more to happen to her or to the
sanctuary.

Though I could not offer much hope for the recovery
of her pigs, I explained to her that whatever happened,
these people would not get away with the theft. The law
of the universe says that what you give out you get back,

so the men who caused Salise's heartache would have heart-aches of their own to deal with one day.

Though I worked very closely with my guides, trying to find the pigs was almost an impossible task. I did not know how long the van had travelled or where it had gone. Madonna had not been able to look out and see any landmarks. I felt very saddened. There was only a slight chance of getting the pigs back.

The good thing was that the press was covering the pig-napping closely, so every few days there would be an update. The people who had stolen the pigs didn't think for a minute that the press would pick up this story. They were going to have difficulty getting rid of their captives.

During the course of the next week, I continued to pick up the pigs' energy. I also asked my guides to bring in some information on the physical level about the pigs' location, which they did. But we were no closer to finding Salise's pigs than we had been at the beginning. We all continued to pray, and many of my friends and clients were praying, too.

Two weeks later Salise had a desperate call from a lady who had bought a baby pig from a pet shop. The woman said the pig was so small she didn't know how to feed it. She was afraid the piglet was dying. Salise told her to bring the pig to Special Pals, not knowing whether it was one of her pigs or not.

Salise and I stayed in contact over the phone. After I connected to the baby pig, I knew it was one of hers, but could not get any information on the rest of the family. Salise named the little pig Wilbur. She nursed him back to health, and he quickly became the darling of Special Pals.

Even the other animals seemed to acknowledge that Wilbur
was special.

Wilbur

Wilbur goes to the animal sanctuary each day, and at night
he stays with Mary Schweiger, a member of the Special
Pals board of directors. He's wiggled his way into all our
hearts and I see him regularly. He is a very superior pig;
in fact, he doesn't believe he is a pig at all. Salise laughs
whenever I say this, but I believe Wilbur was a nobleman
in a former life, because he conducts himself with such
dignity and strength of purpose.

Wilbur's greatest friend is a beautiful German Shepherd
named George who has appointed himself Wilbur's
guardian. George sleeps on the bed with Wilbur every night
at Mary's house. When they arrive at the sanctuary in the
morning with Mary, George stands in front of Wilbur and
protects him from the other dogs, particularly new dogs
who may not yet be aware of Wilbur's importance.

This happy state of affairs continued for a while. Whenever I went to visit Wilbur the first thing I felt was a cold
wet nose pushing against my leg. As I sat down, he would
jump right up my back and start nuzzling me with his
strong nose as he squealed with joy.

Then one morning Salise called and left a frantic message
on my answering machine saying Wilbur had been stolen
again. She was devastated. I let the answering machine play
my other messages as I tried to think of what to do. Before
I could even formulate a plan of action, a new message

from Salise informed me that Wilbur had been found. She was deliriously happy.

I phoned Salise straight away and she proceeded to tell me about Wilbur's latest adventure, and what an adventure it was!

Mary had got up early that morning to take two dogs to the vet for minor surgical procedures. Normally she fed all the animals together but, since the dogs would be undergoing anaesthesia, they couldn't be fed. Though Wilbur was ravenous, she gave him only a dish of plain oats that she knew the dogs would ignore, to avoid problems of jealousy or hurt feelings. She planned to supplement the pig's oat snack with a full meal while the dogs were in surgery.

Naturally Wilbur accompanied Mary and the two dogs to the vet. Though Wilbur didn't need veterinary attention, he liked to be included in all the outings. Mary loaded the three animals in the back of her pick-up and started her journey. She arrived at the vet and went in with the two dogs, Wilbur following close on her heels. Mary told Wilbur to wait in the waiting room and not to move as she took the dogs for their treatment.

By now Wilbur was well past his accustomed breakfast time and his stomach was rumbling. So, Wilbur being a very determined pig (not to mention hungry), he opened the door of the clinic while the receptionist was otherwise occupied and went on his way.

Twenty minutes later Mary came out and found the waiting room empty . . . no Wilbur. The receptionist had no idea where he might have gone. Since Mary is a professional animal rescuer, she knew the first thing to do was

call Animal Control and alert them to the fact that Wilbur
was on the loose.

As it happened, Animal Control had just received an
urgent call from a nearby country club saying they had a
most unusual guest. A gentleman playing golf had been
amazed at the speed with which Wilbur went racing across
the course to the clubhouse, attracted by the enticing aroma
wafting from the buffet line in the main dining room. The
hungry pig, after being treated to the best food any pig
has ever been fed, decided he also wanted eggs for breakfast
and where better to get them than a posh country club?
His arrival in the dining room caused quite a stir, but to
Wilbur it was perfectly normal as he was always in the
dining room at Mary's house when her family ate and, in
fact, often ate with them. He was used to having the best
of everything.

Without waiting to be seated, Wilbur cut in ahead of
most of the guests in the queue and helped himself to the
eggs and buttered toast in the buffet. He was quite a sight,
standing on his hind legs in the buffet line, his snout
pushed down into the breakfast entrees. Though the staff
didn't quite know how to handle Wilbur, they were more
amused than alarmed by his sudden appearance.

Soon, though, the game was up. Mary arrived looking a
bit stern, ready to take Wilbur back to Special Pals. But
the normally outgoing pig wouldn't quite look her in the
eye. He knew he shouldn't have gone off like he did,
especially as he'd been stolen once before. He hadn't meant
to worry her but he'd been hungry, and it wasn't every day
a pig got a chance to dine with the finest members of
Houston society.

Mary picked Wilbur up, but he hadn't finished his breakfast so he wasn't amenable to the idea of leaving yet. He squealed in protest. The dining staff indicated it was all right for Mary to put Wilbur down. The damage had already been done and what was another four eggs or so? Besides, the guests seemed to be amused at the idea of a pig dining in their midst.

Mary put Wilbur down and he finished up the eggs. From then on, Mary learned not to delay Wilbur's mealtimes by even a few minutes, for fear that he would find a way to feed himself.

Sadly, since this adventure, Mary has passed away in a tragic accident. Though I miss her terribly, and the wonderful work she did for Special Pals, I know she is working even harder to help animals now that she has passed over. Wilbur and George especially miss her company, but Salise has given them a loving home at Special Pals.

Foxy

One early winter morning in 1995, I noticed a little black animal outside, lying down and scratching itself. At first, I thought it was Wellington, my cat, then realized he had too much common sense to be out in the cold and rain when he had a nice warm house to stay in. So I went downstairs and saw that it was a little black dog no bigger than my Wellington, in fact even a bit smaller than my well-fed feline.

I noticed the dog seemed frightened and cold, and was obviously hungry. She was very nervous as I approached, and ready to bolt, so I turned back towards my house, all the while sending the communication that everything was all right. I told her telepathically that she was not to worry or be scared, but should follow me back to my house where she would get a dish of food and a treat. As I got up to my back door, I turned my head slightly and could see the little dog was following me, but very slowly as she was shivering so much that she had trouble walking.

I help many abandoned or lost dogs to find new homes, so I brought this one into my house as a matter of course. I gave her food and water right outside the back door, but every time I approached her, she backed off. She obviously did not want to come into a strange house. I walked away to give her time to get used to her new surroundings. Finally, I went back into the lounge and got down flat on my stomach on the floor so that I would appear to be on the same level with the dog, closer to her own size and therefore less intimidating. This is a trick that often works to calm frightened animals.

She wanted to come into the house but she was scared. She would walk up to the door, then back away. I decided to go upstairs and get a blanket to make a nest for the dog so she would at least have a warm and dry place to get into. I left the back door open a bit so the small dog could get inside. She was still dripping wet. I hoped she would climb into the bed I'd made for her and rest.

I came downstairs about an hour later and sure enough, there she was, all curled up in the bed resting. But when she heard me coming she looked at me and made as if to move back outside. I talked to her gently, reassuring her that she was safe. I lay down on my stomach again, stretched out my hand towards her and started transmitting to her that everything was fine; she could come in and she would be warm and safe with us. I assured her she wasn't going to be hurt, but she already seemed to know that.

The little dog scampered into the house with all the enthusiasm of the puppy that she was. She started running all around and shaking herself off, then she came up to me and let me pet her. I went to get a towel to dry the little dog off. I kept the door to the upstairs rooms closed because of Bella and Wellington. I didn't want my other pets to frighten the little dog or to be frightened of her. I picked her up and towelled her until she was dry.

By this time the dog was beginning to feel a bit more at home, so I let her come upstairs to meet Bella, Fitz, Emma and Wellington. I named the dog Foxy because she looked just like a black fox. Though I was a bit worried about jealousy at first, my beloved Rhodesian Ridgeback, Bella, loved the little dog and was happy to have her with us. Fitz and Emma just rolled their eyes, but soon they were as taken as I was with Foxy. Fitz now affectionately calls her 'the little monster'. My cat Wellington was, of course, unmoved, believing the existing balance of one cat and one dog was the correct one. But he, too, has succumbed to the charm of our black pup.

Foxy wanted to play with everyone, but the older animals were not amused. Bella was more curious than anything else. Wellington was most disgusted and asked me, 'What's this thing coming in here?'

I tried to find Foxy's owner by advertising in the paper, but no one came forward. I looked everywhere to see if anyone had put any posters out, but had no luck. So I decided to find a new home for Foxy. Unfortunately, the pup wasn't house-trained. Before I could find a new home for her, I had to get Foxy trained.

I knew the small dog had been traumatized because I could not get her to communicate. Animals that have been badly treated sometimes do not speak for two to three weeks after arriving in a new home. I wanted to find out more about Foxy, so I decided to work through Bella, because the little dog had begun to make herself at home and become friends with Bella.

I heard of a lady who had lost her dog, but she was travelling and wouldn't be back for another few days. I had another homeless dog due to arrive that evening so I didn't have much time to make arrangements for Foxy. Lois, one of the animal foster parents I work with regularly, said she would be happy to foster Foxy for a few days to make room in my house for the other little stray dog that had been found wandering alongside a road with no tag.

The day came when Foxy would have to go. Though she had spent the week destroying my house, chewing up everything and making messes everywhere, she had already managed to worm her way into the hearts of everyone in my home.

I could see that Bella was sad to learn Foxy was going. She had found a little friend she really liked and now that friend was leaving. I explained we had to do this so we could help another little lost dog. I put Foxy in the car and drove her to Lois's office. Lois was expected shortly, and the secretary said I could leave Foxy with her until Lois arrived. I had another appointment so I had no choice but to leave her with the secretary. I felt relieved because the girl was a great dog lover and immediately put Foxy on her knee and cuddled her while she answered the telephone. I felt comfortable that Foxy was in good hands.

The day passed quickly as I was busy with animals and clients. When I saw that it was almost three, I decided to call Lois to see how our little orphan was. To my horror, Lois told me Foxy had got out of the office when some clients came in. By the time I got there, the entire office was looking for Foxy. She'd been sighted but every time anyone got close, she would run away. It was getting cold and dark, and I was feeling frantic. I felt so bad about Foxy being lost again so soon after I had found her.

Charlotte, Lois's secretary, was driving around praying to find Foxy. Finally, she spotted the little dog about two miles away from the office, running across a busy road. Charlotte said Foxy just darted through the traffic. I think she must have borrowed a few of Wellington's nine lives that day. Charlotte tried to call Foxy but she wouldn't come because she was too afraid. I quickly went with Lois and we followed Charlotte to the last spot where Foxy had been seen and started to call her name. But I worried because Foxy had had her new name for only a week, and still didn't respond reliably to a summons. I called and called, feeling quite distraught. I couldn't bear the thought of Foxy being lost once and then within a week being lost again. She was such a little soul, frightened and bewildered.

Sometimes it is difficult to trust my instincts when I am emotionally involved in a case. I was very emotionally involved with Foxy and knew I had to relax if I was going to help her. We'd been looking for almost five hours, but I decided to give it another half hour. By this time, it was

nearly dark and getting bitterly cold. I walked deeper into
the woods by the side of the road and shouted Foxy's name
at the top of my lungs, but to no avail. I was really
panicking. I prayed for Foxy to please hear my voice. As I
walked back to Lois and Charlotte who were also calling
Foxy, I happened to look behind me and there, running at
about a hundred miles an hour, was this little black ball of
fur. She jumped straight up into my arms and I was
overjoyed. I found myself sitting on the ground sobbing
with joy.

Foxy was licking me all over and for the first time she
communicated. I heard her say, 'I knew you would come
for me!' That's what really broke my heart. I explained that
I'd had to leave her and she quite understood. I told her I
would take her home and keep her a bit longer until I could
find her a new home. I reasoned that maybe it was for the
best because Foxy was still not completely house-trained.
When I called Fitz and asked if I could bring her back, he
was so upset he said, 'You must bring her back immediately.'
I think he had already fallen in love with her.

When I brought her home that evening, Foxy had quite
a reception from Bella and even old Wellington, but nothing
like what Foxy got from Fitz. We told ourselves it was only
temporary, that we'd give her a lot more love just until we
could find her a permanent home. But even then, I think I
knew we could never give her up for adoption again.

When I took her to the vet to get her jabs the next day,
he said she was only six to seven months old, and a fine
specimen of a breed I was not familiar with, a 'Schipperke',
or Dutch Captain's Boat Dog. The vet said he knew some-
body who would love to have Foxy for breeding purposes,

and he assured us the family would provide a good home. Fitz and I looked at each other and said almost together, 'No, she's not ready to go yet!' (I'm sure we'll still be saying that in ten years' time.)

That evening Bella told me that Foxy had had a very sad life. Foxy still couldn't communicate well because she was so confused and upset, but Bella was able to make out more of what she was saying than I could. Bella told me that Foxy's mummy (meaning her human mum) threw her out into the street, and she had walked her feet raw looking for a new home. She'd been kept in a cage in the back garden by her unfeeling first owners, who never talked to her, which made her very sad. Foxy missed her dog mummy very much, because she was so young when she was taken away from her.

While Bella was alive, there was only just enough room in our four-poster bed for all of us, as Bella was rather large and took up a lot of space. I got used to sleeping with Bella on one side and Foxy on the other. In her determined fashion, she had stolen all our hearts.

Foxy brought joy into all our lives, but especially to Bella, who enjoyed having a canine companion in the last months of her life.

Kiwi

My friend Helen Stroud called to tell me that one of her cats, Kiwi, was missing. Kiwi was so named because Helen's youngest child had trouble pronouncing 'Kitty'. It came out 'Kiwi' instead.

I first met Helen when she called me to do some healing on Kiwi. The cat had a rather dramatic start in life. Shortly after Helen and her family found the abandoned kitten, our area suffered a devastating flood. Helen's family and pets survived the trauma of rising water together, but after the flood, Kiwi had fallen ill.

Kiwi's illness was due as much to stress and trauma as anything else. After I sent her some healing energy, she bounced right back and had been fine ever since. Now she was lost, and Helen was frantic. She had searched the neighbourhood with no luck, and her children were absolutely devastated.

I connected to Kiwi's energy and got the feeling the cat wasn't too far away, perhaps even in Helen's garden. But she wasn't lost at all; she was hiding out by choice. I asked Kiwi for a description of her location and she sent me a picture of flat, grey rocks stacked up, with soil behind them. She said the steps to the house were nearby though she couldn't tell me whether it was the front or back of the house as animals make no such distinctions. She also sent me a picture of a very large, dense shrub, and I sensed that this was where she was hiding, under the shrub in Helen's garden. I relayed this information to Helen and she told me she had a rock border around a garden near her front door. She went and looked for Kiwi there, and called and called, but caught no glimpse of her pet. Still, I knew this was where the cat was hiding, so I told Helen to put out food and water.

I suggested that if Helen would give her a day or two, Kiwi would probably calm down and come home on her own. But even as I said it, I could feel Kiwi clamouring to communicate, so I asked why she was camped out in the garden, hiding from her loving family. When I asked the cat what was wrong, she poured out a tale of jealousy and intrigue.

Kiwi told me there was another cat in the household, Annabel, who was the favourite of Helen's husband, Dan. Because of this lofty position, Annabel lorded it over the other cats in the house and was quite mean to Kiwi. When I connected to Annabel, she told me she thought Kiwi's skittishness was foolish, and made fun of the nervous cat whenever the opportunity presented itself. And she was always rubbing Kiwi's nose in the fact that the master preferred her to Kiwi.

Just that morning, Annabel had hissed and spat at Kiwi, and tried to slash her across the nose. When Dan heard the commotion, he scolded Kiwi but not Annabel, which had sorely wounded Kiwi's feelings. On top of all this, Helen's house was full of activity because she and Dan were preparing for a holiday party that evening. Kiwi overheard Dan asking that all the pets be put out before the guests arrived. The beautiful grey cat had had enough. She decided to put herself out, permanently. She was determined to see her plan through, but she was also very scared.

As Kiwi and I communicated, Helen's other cats came through. As Kiwi had mentioned, Annabel was imperious, and very proud of her position as the master's favourite. Surprisingly, though, Annabel was not the only cat in Helen's household who was exasperated with Kiwi. 'She's too nervous,' they all chorused. 'She won't come down when guests are here and is always hiding in the cupboard, which is silly, because Helen and her children are very kind to us.'

I discovered all the cats had been in the flood together. They had willingly tolerated Kiwi's skittishness for a few months after the catastrophe, but now they were out of patience with her.

This was going to be a complex case. Just as we get along better with some people than others, so do animals form intricate social communities based on a spirit of mutual co-operation. If one dog or cat or bird or hamster or horse doesn't fit in, then that animal will be shunned by the others. This apparently was what had happened to Kiwi. No wonder she wanted to leave.

Two days after Kiwi's disappearance, Helen went shopping. As she turned into her driveway, she thought she caught a glimpse of Kiwi bounding across the lawn into the front garden. But by the time Helen parked her car and ran back, there was no trace of the cat.

I connected to Kiwi again and she told me the other cats in the house had told her to stop being silly and come back inside. 'But I am too scared,' Kiwi told me. 'There are a lot of wheels going by and noise, and I don't want to move from this safe place.'

Now that Helen knew Kiwi was in the front garden, she had taken to leaving her front door open during the day, hoping the frightened cat would see it and dash inside. She had the door propped open with a large can of peas. Kiwi sent me a picture of the door with the canned peas shining in the sun next to it, but she still had no intention of leaving her sanctuary.

Helen had me tell Kiwi that she would leave open the door of a stone potting shed that connected to the house in the rear. I told Kiwi if she waited until it was dark, she could sneak around the house, go through the shed and right up the back stairway. But Kiwi was beginning to enjoy her new home. She could watch the birds and small animals, and didn't have to endure the taunts of her fellow felines. Kiwi loved Helen and her children very much, but would not go back inside the house because of the situation with the other cats. Helen left food outdoors for a number of months without ever seeing Kiwi, and provided a warm shelter. At first the other cats felt odd about Kiwi being out in the garden, but eventually everyone got used to the situation.

I must say, in the years I have been helping to recover lost animals, I have never had a story with such an unusual conclusion. Kiwi moved outdoors in December 1994, and lived there several months. Then one day when I tried to connect to her energy, it wasn't there any more, and I knew she had passed over. Helen was very sad when I told her the news, but knows that Kiwi has gone to a much better place.

Most lost pet stories do not have happy conclusions. It is best to do everything in your power to prevent your pet from becoming lost in the first place. You must be vigilant about its safety and make sure it has a secure place to stay, especially if it is spending long hours unsupervised outdoors. Make sure your animal is wearing proper ID tags with its name and your phone number displayed. If your dog or cat has a tendency to 'lose' collars, secure the ID tags to a body harness. Otherwise, whoever finds your dog or cat has no way of knowing who the animal belongs to. They may adopt your pet themselves or take it to a pound, where it stands a very good chance of being killed. Either way, you won't see your pet again.

If your pet is lost, contact your local animal welfare centre or shelter immediately. The RSPCA (01403 264181) and Cats Protection League (01403 221900) have a number of shelters across the country. In London, there is the famous Battersea Dogs Home (0171 622 3626). These three organizations have a policy NEVER to kill healthy animals, and will only put an animal down because of injury or illness. Your Yellow Pages will also have local listings. Most shelters recommend visiting every three days. I say go EVERY day. Some local shelters are so overcrowded that putting animals down is the only way to accommodate others.

By law, all local authorities have to provide a means of dealing with stray animals. Most do this through dog wardens (who actually handle all strays) and pounds, or an environmental officer. Note, however, that your pet is much more likely to be destroyed if it does not go to a shelter.

Put up posters with your pet's picture in the area where they disappeared. Remember that lost animals tend to stay on the move because they are looking for their home. Dogs can cover ten to fifteen miles a day in their search, and cats hitch rides in service vehicles, so don't confine your search to the area immediately around your home, but work outward as the days go by, to keep up with your pet's possible progress. I have recovered animals as far as fifty miles away from their original location.

Perhaps nowhere is the old cliché, 'An ounce of

prevention is worth a pound of cure,' more true than in pet ownership. If you are a diligent and responsible pet owner, you will reduce the chance of ever having to deal with the heartbreak of a lost pet.

One of the most fascinating things about pets is their diverse personalities. It has been no surprise to me, as I have become more and more involved in animal communication, to discover that our pets find us just as fascinating as we find them. You may think no one is around, but your pet is watching you. I share some funny human stories I've been told by animals in the next chapter.

CHAPTER 9

What the butler saw: your pet is watching you

The idea that pets are acute observers of human behaviour is disconcerting to some people. But animals have no malice in them, and the stories they tell of their owners, no matter how embarrassing, are relayed in all innocence.

Think of how you delight in watching your pet, how you enjoy entertaining your friends with stories of his exploits. Does it not make sense that animals would enjoy the same thing, swapping stories of their owners back and forth?

You'll recall from the first chapter of this book that as a child in Hartwell, England, I was privy to every secret in our village, courtesy of my inquisitive animal friends. Trying to determine the source of my intelligence regularly confounded my parents. The truth that I told them, that my animal friends had given me all the gossip, was a truth they simply could not comprehend.

Animals in a neighbourhood often trade stories about what is going on with their owners' families, and how their owners treat them. My client Nancy saw her dog take a piece of chicken she had just been given and carry it in her mouth to the dog next door, who was neglected by its owners and often went unfed. I know the poor hungry dog had telepathically sent a message to Nancy's dog, saying it hadn't been fed and was hungry, and could she spare a bit of that nice chicken it was smelling? Nancy's dog was generous and kind-hearted, and so well taken care of by Nancy that it didn't mind sharing. But remember that animals have different personalities just as we humans do. Another dog might not have been so willing to share.

Both domesticated and wild animals communicate with each other, and are likely to exchange information and warnings. For example, when my co-author Pat showed herself sympathetic to wildlife, she experienced a positive invasion of furry creatures in her large and heavily wooded back garden. Pat and I know it was because the animals had telepathically transmitted a message throughout the wood saying she was a kind and friendly human. Actually, many of the animals were probably already in residence, but didn't feel emboldened to show themselves until they were certain it was safe.

I'm sure many of you have seen homes where cats seem to congregate. You can be sure when you see such a house that the cats have been telling each other there was a feline-loving human in residence at that address. I've been told that sick raccoons present themselves regularly at the animal shelter here in Montgomery County Texas. It is because they know that is where they can get help and volunteers at the animal shelter are constantly putting out pictures and feelings of helping animals. Animals in the area surrounding the shelter receive these pictures telepathically. They feel the positive energy coming from the shelter, so they use their senses as a sort of built-in compass to find help.

Though wild animals certainly watch us with the same interest as our pets do, the funniest stories I've been told about humans come to me from domesticated pets. Since these stories are potentially embarrassing, I've left out the names of the humans involved, and changed the names and identifying characteristics of the pets. So if you think you recognize yourself here, it's just coincidental.

Dabney and Eliza

A couple came to consult me because their two Golden Retrievers, Dabney and Eliza, were getting out of the bedroom each night and wrecking the house. Just that morning they had awakened to discover the corner of the coffee table chewed, cushions torn from the sofa, and a vase of flowers knocked over and broken. They asked me to find out why their dogs wouldn't stay in the bedroom with them at night as they were instructed to do, and why they were so destructive.

The answer to the destruction was easy. When animals are bored and unsupervised, they often go on rampages that result in severe damage to clothing, furniture and knick-knacks. They don't see it as naughty; to them it is simply play.

When I connected to the two dogs, I found them quite affable. I asked why they wouldn't stay in the bedroom. Before they could reply, I began to experience quite an unpleasant sensation in my nose. Although the dogs knew their owners were upset with their disobedience, they transmitted with pictures and feelings the clear message that they simply could not stay in that bedroom. I wondered if their desire to escape was related to the sudden sensitivity in my nose.

Nonetheless, I was quite stern with the dogs. 'You know you must stay in the bedroom,' I told them.

'But we can't!' came the plaintive answer once again.

I knew there was more to it than they were telling me. After quite a bit of prodding, I discovered their human father had a chronic case of nocturnal intestinal gas and the dogs' noses were sensitive to this. Things were fine for the first thirty minutes or so after the humans went to bed. The dogs behaved nicely and everyone fell asleep. But once the nightly eructations started, they felt compelled to escape the room quickly, an escape made possible by Dabney's clever turning of the L-shaped handle on the bedroom door.

Not wishing to cause my clients embarrassment, I simply told them that the dogs had requested their own bedroom, which they had not, and asked if they had another room the dogs could sleep in. Since the couple's children were grown and they lived in a large house, the request was simple to fulfil. I suggested they furnish the selected room with toys and chewies to keep their playful pets occupied and out of trouble. I also hinted that they might find it wise to change the style of the door handle in that room, to keep Dabney from effecting an escape.

Once the retrievers were moved into their own room full of interesting toys, and not subjected every night to the noxious smells produced by their father, the owners informed me that the midnight rampages stopped and all was peaceful once more in their home.

Still, I can't help but wonder how the man's wife slept through all that. Perhaps she was blessed with a poor sense of smell, or maybe she slept with a nose plug.

Teddy and Matilda

One day, I was consulted by a lady who told me that she and her husband were distraught because their two seven-year-old pure-bred cats were suddenly having accidents all over the house: on the sofa, on the rug, even on the bed. The problem was particularly puzzling because the cats had always been perfectly behaved. The husband was so angry about their ruined carpet and furniture that he told his wife she must correct the problem immediately or get rid of the cats. There would be no compromise. (It will perhaps give you some insight into this man's character to know that he decided his wife alone had to solve their joint problem, and that insight may help explain his wife's behaviour later in this story.)

He seemed to be the sort of man who loved his wife and cats well, as long as they did just what he wanted them to do. But any deviation from his programme was excuse enough to get rid of the cats. Perhaps his wife felt her position was tenuous as well. As you will soon see, the problem really was more the wife's than the husband's.

The couple lived in a Southern Colonial mansion in one of the most elegant areas of Houston. Their home was filled with priceless antiques and artifacts, prized possessions the cats were eliminating, one by one. The lady begged for my help. She loved her cats and did not want them to be put aside for the sake of a piece of furniture.

When I connected to her two cats, they immediately assured me that they loved their 'mummy and daddy' (as animals often refer to their owners), but really didn't like that new man Mummy had started bringing home in the afternoon.

I realized immediately the lady had taken a lover. I also knew I'd discovered the answer to the puzzle, the obvious source of the cats' upset.

I decided to get a bit more information from the cats, and invited them to continue their story. They went on to complain that their mummy had the nerve to pitch them out of 'their' bedroom, the one they had always shared with their owners, and then she closed the door, shutting them out. Feeling somewhat put out by this lack of regard for their rights, they responded in the time-honoured tradition of scorned pets everywhere. They started making messes all over the house. They deliberately picked the most open and obvious spots to deposit their 'accidents', which were no accident at all, to let their owners know how displeased they were with the recent turn of events.

The lady must have noticed my amused look and realized something was wrong. I told her what the cats had just relayed to me, and then it was her turn to be surprised.

'I can't believe they knew I had taken a lover,' she said.

'They know everything,' I told her.

'But what shall I tell my husband?' she asked.

I informed her I didn't give that sort of advice; all I could do was tell her how to deal with her cats. But I did suggest that perhaps it would be wiser to meet her lover elsewhere, to avoid upsetting the cats. I felt that alone would restore tranquillity to the domestic life of her cats. How to restore tranquillity to the domestic life of the woman was another matter entirely.

The woman left my studio in something of a state and I knew I would never see her again. But I am sure she never thought when she brought her lover home that it would affect her cats so dramatically, or that they would soon be telling her deepest secret to me.

Buster

A client came to my office very concerned because her eight-year-old Border Collie's coat was falling out. There hadn't been a change in Buster's diet; he didn't have fleas or a skin inflammation. Her vet had thoroughly examined the dog and could find nothing wrong.

When I tuned in to Buster, I discovered a very cheerful dog who told me he knew his mummy was coming to see me, and had been waiting for me to speak to him. Buster even told me why his mummy was consulting me; she was worried about his coat. Then he told me his hair was falling out just like his daddy's. This gave me my first clue to the problem.

I asked the lady if her husband was experiencing hair loss. She answered immediately that he was absolutely obsessive about his receding hairline.

'He stands in front of the mirror and stares at his hair for fifteen minutes every morning,' she told me, 'then asks me if I think any more has fallen out overnight. He's very worried about it.'

I asked her if Buster ever went into the dressing room with his daddy while these conversations were going on. She told me the dog always accompanied her husband during his morning routine. Buster sent me a picture of his daddy working out on an exercise machine, then going into the shower. He told me this was his favourite moment, because he loved getting a spray of water in his face. He said his daddy was very particular about his dress, sometimes changing shirts twice in the morning if he didn't like the way he looked.

My client confirmed that her husband was very fastidious, and was stunned when I told her Buster knew she was sad over losing one of her favourite blue earrings. The chatty dog also mentioned that he much preferred her new bed covering to the old one and wanted to know for certain if she was going to keep it. She couldn't believe her pet was so observant, but we were finding that Buster really had an eye for detail.

I picked up a feeling of extreme worry from Buster. He told me his daddy was very anxious because his hair was falling out, and now his mummy was upset because the dog's hair was beginning to fall out, too.

There was a definite connection between the two problems. Buster had picked up his owner's fear of hair loss. Because he loved his owner so much and strongly identified with him, he started worrying his hair would fall out, too. His worry had grown so all-consuming it became a self-fulfilling prophecy and Buster started to experience a sort of sympathetic baldness, shedding so much hair that he, too, developed bald spots.

Buster asked me if his hair would keep falling out like his daddy's. I promptly told him that dog hair did not fall out like human hair, so he had no need to worry. I told his mummy that Buster was picking up tremendous stress and anxiety from his daddy. His belief that he would become bald like his daddy was so powerful that it was actually making his hair fall out, even though there was no physical reason for the hair loss.

I told my client she must constantly remind Buster that a dog's hair didn't fall out in the same way as a man's, so he needn't worry about such a thing happening. I explained to Buster that his master's anxiety about his inevitable baldness was natural, but that didn't mean that Buster's hair would fall out, too.

I asked the lady to keep me informed of Buster's condition and to tell me if there was any change in his coat. My client returned a month later to say that Buster's hair was growing back, and all the bald patches were covered over. If only I had the same luck in restoring human hair, I should be able to retire in six months!

It is not necessary to go around in a state because you know your pet is watching you. Rather, let it serve as a reminder to be on your best behaviour; to be the best possible pet owner you can be. If you are kind and loving to your pet and treat him with courtesy and respect, then you really have nothing to worry about, because your pet will have only nice things to say about you. If occasionally your pet lets you know with a look that he has caught you in a funny situation, let it go. None of us is perfect.

But you shouldn't have to guess at your pet's thoughts and feelings. With a bit of practice, almost anyone who is open to the idea can learn how to communicate telepathically with animals. In the next chapter, I will give you step-by-step instructions on how to achieve that communication, along with easy exercises you can do to test your ability to reach your pet on the telepathic level. You can build a better relationship with your animal if you just open your mind.

CHAPTER 10

If I could talk to the animals: communicating with your animal

My clients often ask me exactly how I communicate with their pets. But what people are really curious about is whether they themselves can establish telepathic communication with animals. The answer is yes. In this chapter, I will explain the specifics of telepathic communication, which is how I 'talk' to animals, and give step-by-step instructions that will enable many readers to open a channel of telepathic communication with their own pets.

The most important skill you must master before you attempt telepathic communication with your pet is the art of relaxation. Many people find it difficult to meditate or relax. If you follow these basic instructions, you can achieve a state of relaxation relatively quickly. Unplug the phone, turn off the television and radio, lock the door if you have to. If there is a particular piece of soft music you like, listen to that. I like to be still and quiet with no music. You will find what works best for you.

Sit on a comfortable chair or lie on your bed and close your eyes. Concentrate on your breathing and breathe deeply in and out. Bring your awareness to your body. Start to relax your toes and feet. Be aware of the relaxed feeling travelling through your legs and knees up to the top of your legs as you continue to breathe deeply in and out.

Feel the lower half of your body relaxing. Notice the relaxed feeling travelling through your chest and right through to your shoulders, then down through your arms and elbows to your wrists. Feel your hands and fingers relaxing. Feel that relaxation travelling up through your neck and face, relaxing your eyes. Soon your eyes will begin to feel heavy and now your head will be completely relaxed. Be aware of that wonderful feeling travelling throughout your body. Now that you are in a relaxed state, you are ready to start.

No matter how relaxed you are, you will not be successful if your pet is distracted. Animals will not listen if they have other things occupying their attention. Humans are not so different. If you were studying for an exam, your mind would be occupied with your work and not particularly receptive to any other stimuli. You would certainly not want to start a conversation. You would not even be listening.

It is the same with animals, even though their method of communication is telepathic and not verbal. When people tell me their dog won't listen to them, my first thought is, 'What is he doing when you are trying to talk to him?' If he is busy scratching or watching a squirrel through the window, he won't be very interested in anything you have to say; he is already pleasantly occupied.

If you are to have any success in communicating with your pet, either telepathically or verbally, you must wait until your animal is quiet and not distracted by anything else. Make sure your animal has been fed and taken out, and that all his physical needs have been met before you begin. Choose a quiet time and make sure you have your pet's complete attention. Don't worry if your pet is dozing; you can reach him on a telepathic level even if he is sleeping.

Then take your pet to the quiet, peaceful spot you have chosen, relax, clear your mind and begin.

Telepathic communication is not as hard as you might think. I have developed two easy exercises – one for dogs and one for cats – that will give you clear proof that you have reached your animals on a telepathic channel. It's a bit more complex when you try to determine whether or not you have received telepathic communication from your pet, because that involves trusting your imagination and intuition. But we shall come to that later. First, the exercises, which are different for dogs and cats because our most popular domestic pets react best to different stimuli.

Communicating with Your Dog

Either touch your animal or say his name – let's assume your dog is a he – so he will know you want to communicate. Imagine you are going to take your dog out for a walk. (Don't perform this experiment if the weather won't permit a walk, because it is important to fulfil with physical action what we promise our animals on the telepathic level, or else they will learn to distrust us.) Imagine how much fun a walk would be and picture the path you will take, and all the exciting sights and scents your dog might encounter along the way. See yourself running or walking alongside your dog, and feel the exhilarating sense of freedom and the joy of experiencing nature at first hand.

The more you let your feelings and imagination soar, the stronger your communication will be and the better your chance of success. Be confident. You are painting pictures with your feelings and imagination which your pet will see as surely as if you had painted them with a brush on canvas. Remember how you use your imagination in everyday life to create ideas and dreams, to set goals and make plans. That is no different from what I am asking you to do with your pet.

Now, take the pictures and feelings you have created, and use your mind energy to 'toss' them out as you would a ball from your hand. Then watch carefully to see your pet's reaction. If he starts to bark and runs excitedly to where his leash is kept, he has telepathically received the message that you want to take him for a walk, and now it is time to keep your promise. It really is that easy.

Communicating with Your Cat

Since a walk on a leash is not at all appealing to most cats, I've devised a different exercise for them. I suggest you entice cats with a treat. I'll assume your cat is a female. Picture yourself opening a tin of her favourite food: tuna or chicken, whatever it is. Then imagine the tantalizing smell, the delicious taste. Send out the feelings of pleasure your cat will have when you share this treat with her, which will be soon if she shows you by her actions that she has received your message. If your cat starts miaowing and rubbing herself against you, or showing you the behaviour that typically precedes her mealtimes, then you will know you have succeeded.

✳

It is important to preserve the integrity of these experiments by using nothing other than the powers of silent suggestion on your pet. It's not fair to get out the leash or rattle the tin opener, because then the communication is auditory and not telepathic.

When you are attempting telepathic communication with your pet, it is also most important that your body and mind work together. Don't send one message with your mind and another with your physical body. That will confuse your animal and defeat your attempts to communicate. For instance, if you are telling your dog verbally (with your physical body) you want him to be nice to your new cat, but your mental image is of your dog chasing the cat, he is likely to act on the more powerful telepathic picture. Be sure to picture what you want telepathically while you are saying it verbally.

Don't be too disappointed if you do not achieve success the first time you try these tests. Several factors can affect the outcome. If you are not relaxed, calm and focused, your telepathic communication may not be clear. Remember, too, that animals vary in their ability and desire to communicate telepathically. If they are preoccupied with something else when you try these experiments, your pets will not pay much attention to you, novel though your communication attempts may be.

It is my belief that humans are all born with the ability to communicate telepathically. I also believe that if we didn't have the faculty of speech we would all communicate telepathically just as animals do. Everything we need for telepathic communication is already wired into our brains. But our lives are so busy and noisy; we are so preoccupied with our thoughts and the cares of our everyday lives that we don't take the time we need to be quiet and get in touch with our inner senses and our imagination, which are essential steps to access the telepathic channel.

As children, we are very aware of our inner senses. We trust our feelings and imaginations implicitly. Ideally we should continue to trust our imagination as adults, but all too often we discount information that comes from our imagination and tell ourselves it cannot be real. But in order to communicate telepathically with our animals, we must believe in the power of our imaginations and not discount what we are sensing, feeling and hearing. Those feelings, ideas, thoughts and pictures that come to us unbidden when we are relaxed and quiet are actually our animals' way of talking to us. If we shove them away, we are blocking a higher level of communication with our pets that could bring us even closer to them.

You will remember how I told you earlier in this chapter that it was a bit more difficult to determine when an animal has sent a telepathic communication back to us. There is no sure-fire test for this. One of the most important things I tell my clients who are trying to establish telepathic communication with their animals is that they must not dismiss any thought, idea or feeling that comes to them during their attempts to communicate telepathically with their pets, no matter how fantastic it may seem. Rather they should learn to welcome the images and ideas that start flowing to them telepathically, because they contain valuable information that could give them deep insight into their pet's behaviour and personality.

But what exactly is it you are looking for? If you have

sent a telepathic communication to your pet, then suddenly discover an unusual idea or picture forming in your brain, or 'hear' a response 'spoken' inside your head, you have succeeded. Trust your imagination and do not dismiss these unfamiliar images and feelings out of hand. As you become more adept at telepathic communication, you will experience a whole new dimension of joy and awareness and gain an understanding of the animal kingdom that will enhance both your life and that of your animals.

My co-author, Pat, had never had any experience of telepathic communication. But as she spent more time with me and saw the results I was achieving, she decided to try her hand at it and sent out a picture of a tin of tuna to her cat, who was sleeping across the room. Pat concentrated on sending the delicious taste of the tuna, and the feeling of happiness the cat would have while eating the treat. Immediately the cat woke up, bounded across the room and up into Pat's lap, miaowing loudly for the promised treat. Pat was quite taken aback by her quick success.

But don't worry if you don't receive an answer the first few times you communicate. It is a surprise to your pet the first time he hears your telepathic voice and some pets take a while to get used to hearing you on that channel. If you continue to practise, you will eventually succeed.

Keep your sessions brief, about ten minutes or so, as animals have short attention spans and tire quickly. If you drone on, you will lose their attention. Be aware of their body language, as that will give you clear signals about your pets' receptiveness.

Don't keep asking the same question for too long because animals get bored just like people do. If you don't receive an answer, change your question to something else. Try asking if there is anything your pet would like you to do for him. Give him a chance to think about your question. Don't ask more than one question at a time. Accept whatever you receive back, but don't add your thoughts to this feeling or picture. Always acknowledge that your animal has spoken to you. Pet him, thank him and tell him how much you love him.

Seven Simple Steps to Communicating with Your Pet

1 Begin with a calm and tranquil mind and seek out a calm and tranquil atmosphere for you and your animal.

2 Say your animal's name telepathically to get his attention.

3 Visualize your animal as you say his name.

4 Send a picture of his physical body. Direct this to him, along with his name.

5 Ask if there is anything your pet would like you to do for him. Imagine your animal is sending an answer back to you and accept whatever you receive in your imagination.

6 Always acknowledge the answer, whatever you receive back from your animal.

7 Continue to ask him other questions, and remember to trust your imagination for what you are receiving back from your animal.

As your communication skills start to improve, you will find that you no longer have to practise relaxation first. You will find you can use telepathic communication in your everyday life. If you are in your kitchen and have your pets' dinner ready or a treat for them, send the message out telepathically and see how they respond. Send a picture of the dinner and yourself putting it down for them and them eating it. Try these little exercises as you go about your routine and you will be pleasantly surprised to discover how your awareness and telepathic abilities are increasing.

When you have mastered the basics of telepathic communication, you can go a step further. Now that you recognize your animal's language, your intuition is sharpened, so you are using your energy and emotional body to its full capacity. You are not only speaking the animal's language, you are experiencing a whole new world of communication and now you understand there is much more than the faculty of speech to communicate with. You are using your telepathic ability to communicate mentally, physically and spiritually with your animal.

You will find that once your physical body responds, you will start to experience what the animal is feeling. Imagine yourself on all fours, in the same posture as your animal. Your arms are your pet's two front legs, your back legs are their back legs. Maybe you feel pain in your right leg. That would relate to your animal's right hind leg. If you get a pain in your left hand, that might mean your animal's left paw is hurting.

When you start to feel pain or discomfort that you know does not relate to you, don't dismiss it. Your pet may be transmitting any pain he feels in his physical body to your physical body. This ability to communicate physical feelings telepathically will help you to know what is wrong with your animal before your vet does. So now you are not only speaking with your mind energy, you are speaking with your emotional and physical body and your intuition.

If you follow these basic steps of communicating with your animal, many of you will be able to establish a recognizable telepathic link with your pet. Once you are proficient, you will find you don't have to concentrate quite so hard on relaxing; it will begin to come automatically with practice.

If you hope to master telepathic communication, you must learn to trust your feelings and imagination as children do. You must be open so that the feelings and pictures your animals send to you are not discarded out of hand, but examined, interpreted and utilized to enhance communication. Remember to trust your imagination. With practice and concentration, many of you will be able to access the telepathic communication channel your pets use every day.

Whether or not you ever experience telepathic communication with your animal, you can achieve much simply by making sure that all your spoken communications are delivered with love, gentleness and positive energy. In this way, your pet will always be assured of your love and caring, which will go a long way towards eliminating some common behavioural problems before they start.

It is not only domestic pets which can benefit from telepathic communication. In the next chapter, I will share some interesting stories of communication with wild animals.

CHAPTER 11

Howls and whispers: communicating with wild animals

So far we have talked only of domestic pets, but it is also possible to communicate telepathically with wild animals. Though the vast majority of requests for my help concern family pets, I do have cases in my files where clients have asked that I establish communication with a wild or feral animal to help them resolve some problem.

Pat's Raccoons

My co-author, Pat, has provided me with my most fascinating and perhaps longest-running case of telepathic communication with wild animals. One evening in the autumn of 1995, Pat and I were meeting to work on this book and I noticed she looked very tired. When I asked her why, she replied she had been up most of the previous night because of a series of awful noises coming from her attic: crashes, thumps, skittering and scratching. Pat didn't know what was causing the noise, but was afraid her home had been invaded by an army of rats or worse. Her children were even more scared than she was.

I asked if I could use Pat's energy to connect to the nocturnal invaders and immediately sensed that her intruder was a raccoon, a young female. As winter was approaching, I knew the animal was looking for a place to keep warm but I also knew that attics, with their asbestos insulation and electrical wiring, could be very dangerous places for wild animals.

The raccoon said she had been living in a hollow in Pat's back garden that had caved in during a period of heavy rain. Now she was looking for a new home. I asked how she had gained access to Pat's house and she told me there was a rotten place in the wood next to Pat's chimney and she had managed to chew through to the attic. The raccoon told me she could feel the warm air coming through the hole and decided Pat's attic would make a highly suitable winter home.

I told Pat to speak to the raccoon and tell her she must come out of the attic, but I knew she also had to provide the raccoon with an alternative home for the winter or the animal would not leave. She made that very clear to me when I communicated with her. You must always remember, when you move wild animals from one place to another, that you have to provide a suitable habitat for them to move into; otherwise you will have no luck with the transfer.

Though a bit sceptical, that evening Pat took a flashlight, shone it into the hole in her soffit and told the raccoon she must speak to her. To Pat's surprise, the raccoon immediately came out and listened attentively while Pat told her she was welcome on her property, but that she must move to the new house she would provide. She even posed for a picture Pat took to show me. In the meantime, Pat asked the raccoon to be quiet at night, so that she and her children could sleep without interruption. Pat told the raccoon that if she had work to do, she should do it in the early evening, before her family went to sleep.

The raccoon turned and went back into the house. Immediately a commotion broke out and for the next three hours, the raccoon was busy in the attic. Suddenly, all became quiet, and remained quiet all night long. The raccoon kept to this pattern of work in the early evening and quiet all night. Pat decided this arrangement would be satisfactory, and so she lived throughout the winter, with no difficulties from her resident raccoon and no disturbances. She left the hole in the soffit open for the raccoon to come and go.

Considering what happened to Pat and the raccoon the following spring, we now know it would have been better for Pat to have built the raccoon house at this time. But she did not yet know enough about raccoons to design an effective home for them, plus she had some financial considerations that would not have permitted the construction of a suitable habitat at that time.

In the spring of 1996, two rogue male raccoons showed up to court Pat's boarder. Peace and quiet disappeared. I tried communicating with the two males to tell them they must be quieter, but they were in no mood to listen. Their feelings were running high and, just as with humans, raging emotions kept the raccoons from choosing the best path. Their jealousy towards each other and fierce desire to prevail in the mating contest kept them from responding to my reasonable requests to stop being so loud and combative. Pat was falling over with fatigue and her children didn't want to stay at the house because of the noises the raccoons were making all night long.

Finally, one night while Pat and her children were watching television together, a furious fight broke out above them. The rival suitors screeched and hurtled back and forth from one end of Pat's attic to the other. Pat thought the fight would end at any moment but the noise and violence of the conflict kept escalating. Suddenly there was a loud crash in the garage. Pat arrived just in time to see two huge raccoons scramble back up the walls and disappear into a gaping hole they had created when they came plummeting through the garage ceiling, bringing about ten square feet of plasterboard and insulation down with them.

Pat had reached the end of her tether. She called a wildlife removal expert, only to discover there was a quarantine in force in Texas that prohibited the transportation of rabies-susceptible species such as raccoons. In effect, the raccoons could not be removed from Pat's property without breaking the law.

Pat and I discussed what to do. She called a raccoon expert, who advised her to scoop up fresh dog mess every morning and distribute it throughout her attic. The expert said raccoons hated dogs and the smell of the mess would discourage them from staying in the attic. Pat told me she could hardly blame them for that, and worried that the smell might be a bit much for her, too. Nor did she relish the idea of sneaking out in the early hours to collect fresh dog mess each morning. She wasn't certain what this would do to her reputation with her neighbours. So Pat found herself unable to comply with this advice, and asked what else the expert would recommend.

Pat was then advised to spray her attic with ammonia each evening, once again working on the noxious smell theory. The ammonia did chase off the raccoons, but they always returned as soon as the smell evaporated. The next recommendation was to play loud, obnoxious rock music in the attic, but it did nothing to disturb the raccoons, and kept Pat and her children more awake than ever.

Pat then bought some vinyl-coated steel mesh. The next time the raccoons left the attic, she nailed the rigid metal mesh over the hole, sealing it completely. She put a humane trap baited with the raccoons' favourite cat food in the attic in case one or more of the raccoons was still inside the house. That evening, she heard the trap spring shut and discovered she had captured a large raccoon. Because of the rabies quarantine, the wildlife experts told Pat the only thing she could legally do with the raccoon was to release it on her property, so the next morning Pat let the raccoon loose in her back garden and he hightailed it for the nearest tree.

A couple of peaceful months went by, then Pat once again heard scratching in the ceiling of her bedroom, near where the original entrance hole had been. When she investigated the next morning, she saw that the steel-reinforced mesh had been bent back as if it was a piece of cardboard. The raccoons were inside.

I connected to them through Pat's energy and found just the one female I had communicated with originally. She told me she was pregnant and her babies were due any day. She needed a place to raise her litter. Pat is too kind-hearted for her own good sometimes, so she agreed to let the raccoon mother stay if she would keep quiet. There were not too many other options available to her because of the quarantine.

Another couple of peaceful months went by, then the babies left the nest and started wrestling and chasing each other all over the attic. Since they were infants, they were not very responsive to my requests that they behave themselves.

The weather grew warm and, while Pat and I were still trying to figure out what to do, her house became unusually hot. Pat called a contractor who discovered that the raccoons, to relieve their own discomfort in the Texas heat, had sliced open the air-conditioning ducts in Pat's attic, and were living in pleasant coolness above while she and her children sweltered below. Both Pat and I were incredulous, but the contractor insisted that raccoons frequently 'air-conditioned' attics to maintain their own summertime comfort. He said he had seen many such examples of raccoon intelligence and inventiveness in the course of his work.

Pat had another shock when she phoned her insurance company. The raccoons had caused more than five thousand dollars in damage during their nine-month stay, but the actuary assured Pat her case was not unusual. She said raccoon damage was the number one cause of homeowner claims in our area.

Pat rented the humane trap again, unhappy that such traps, while securing the animal without injury, can hold only one animal at a time. She knew there was a family in her attic, but hoped that if she released them all in the same area, they would find each other again. Then Pat and her family would finally have some peace of mind, and a house free of ongoing damage and constant, all-night noise from the raccoons.

Over the course of the next three weeks, Pat trapped the adult female and two of her babies, old enough at that point to be called juveniles. After checking to make sure the raccoon mother was no longer nursing, Pat released her in a park close to a lake, which she hoped would ensure an abundant source of food and water. Pat told me the mother sang a woeful, trilling song when she was released, a noise unlike anything Pat had ever heard from a raccoon's throat. I knew the raccoon was heartbroken because she was being taken from her babies, but she was no more heartbroken than Pat, who was suffering agonies of guilt over what she was doing.

As I mentioned earlier, Pat had planned to release the babies in the same spot as the mother, in the hope that the family would be reunited in the wild. But it was several days before the first juvenile went into the trap. In the interim, we had a heavy rain which washed away all traces of the adult female's scent, so the babies wouldn't have been able to track their way to their mother.

After she trapped the first juvenile, Pat sought the advice of the Texas Wildlife Center, who told her that releasing such a young animal in the wild, even in the same area as its mother had just been released, would be an almost certain death sentence. Raccoons stay with their mother for at least a year while she teaches them to hunt and protect themselves from their natural predators such as owls, hawks, dogs and humans. These babies were old enough to provide themselves with an adequate if somewhat limited diet, but their mother had not yet taught them all the lessons they needed to learn in order to survive and live a normal life span in the wild.

In addition to rabies, there was an epidemic of distemper among raccoons in our area, and the experts, though legally unable to ask Pat to bring the juvenile to them, strongly suggested they would know best how to deal with it. So Pat took them the darling little animal, knowing full well she was breaking the 'law' but not having any other choice. She had to get the raccoons out of her attic as quickly as possible so she could have repairs made and secure her home once again.

The people at the centre are dedicated to wildlife, and value wild animal interests more highly than human convenience, as well they should. They told Pat that raccoon habitats are rapidly being destroyed by urban sprawl and overbuilding, and the animals have no choice but to invade homes during the cold winter months so they can survive and stay warm. Pat felt sad that the raccoons' natural habitat had collapsed, but knew she could no longer share her attic with them.

There are several remarkable things about this story. One is the responsiveness of the adult female raccoon to telepathic communication. Every time we asked her to calm down, she did so immediately. And yet the adult males, in the throes of springtime passion, ignored our pleas for consideration. The babies, too, were difficult to instruct, because they were so little and playful.

Pat believes, as I do, that we all have a responsibility to care and provide for animals; that they have as much right to be here as we humans do. She knew raccoon habitats were being destroyed, but did not know why they were

invading so many homes in our area, which is heavily
forested. Pat thought there should have been plenty of
potential raccoon homes available in the many large trees
growing all around us.

When she started investigating, Pat discovered the reason
the raccoons had chosen her home instead of one of the
dozens of mature trees in her back garden is that raccoons
cannot live out in the open. They must have a protected
shelter in which to sleep, pass the winter and raise babies.
This information got Pat thinking . . . If raccoon damage
was the number one cause of homeowner insurance claims
in our area, then raccoons must be responsible for damaging
homes in other areas also.

Pat came up with the idea of developing an artificial
'coon hollow' which homeowners could attach to a tree in
their garden to attract raccoons. Admittedly it would not
be heated or air-conditioned but, if properly designed, it
could prevent problems for many homeowners while pro-
viding raccoons with a suitable place to live. Once Pat has
a prototype of her coon hollow available for testing, I'm
sure we will have many more raccoon stories to share.

Some people, whose first response to the raccoon invasion
would have been to put out poison or get a shotgun, might
think Pat went a bit overboard. To these people I say that
every animal was put here by God for a reason. They all
have a vital role in the ecological balance of our earth and
when we start trying to play God, without regard for the
innate balance that exists in all of nature, we get into real
trouble.

History is full of stories of ecological disasters that have
occurred when humans have recklessly altered the balance

of nature to satisfy their own needs of the moment. Before we decide to eliminate a raccoon, we should consider that they kill and eat poisonous snakes, yellowjackets, grubs, larvae of many insects destructive to our crops and ornamental shrubbery, slugs, carpenter and fire ants, carpenter bees and many types of destructive beetles. Yes, raccoons, birds and other wild animals may occasionally spoil some of our garden vegetables, but remember the old poem:

> One for the birds
> One for the bees
> One for the Good Lord
> And one for me.

I've never known a person who could eat all the vegetables they grew in their gardens, so why not share your abundant harvest with wild animals? Humans do not hold an exclusive right to exploit the earth's bounty for their needs alone. The fruits of the earth were put here for animals to enjoy too.

Human beings are destroying wildlife habitat at a terrifying rate. Where are wild creatures supposed to live if we bulldoze all their trees and hollows? What are they supposed to eat? It is incredible so many wild animals have adapted and learned to live close to us. If we don't make accommodations for the animal kingdom in our planning, then we are dooming ourselves to future problems, and perhaps even signing the planet's death certificate. Maintaining a proper ecological balance and learning to co-exist in peaceful abundance with all the earth's creatures are absolutely essential if the human race is to survive.

Repairs to Pat's home were scheduled, but the story hadn't ended. Pat was very concerned that there were still two juveniles in her attic. The second one she had taken to the Wildlife Center had tested positive for distemper. I connected with the babies and sent them a picture of walking into the trap side by side. I told them that if they did that, they could stay together in a lovely house Pat was having built in her garden.

The next morning, Pat called me very excited. The two babies were in the trap. The carpenter rushed to complete the raccoon house, then Pat painted it and moved the babies into their new home.

Now, every night around nine thirty, they come out on their raised porch to eat and drink, then they are off to explore the neighbourhood. But their habitat no longer includes Pat's home, because she has a solid new roof. Acting on the advice of Mona Miller, who has cared for injured and orphaned raccoons for many years, Pat also sprayed a mixture of dog and human hair throughout her attic. In the unlikely event of the raccoons breaking in again, the scent of the hair will act as a danger signal and chase them away, and keep them from settling in.

Rutger Hauer

Pat has been so taken up with her raccoon experiences and her decision to try to develop a coon hollow that she tells her story frequently. A friend of hers, Stephanie, had been having difficulty with an aggressive hummingbird who was trying to control access to all seven hummingbird feeders in her back garden. She nicknamed him Rutger Hauer after the famous actor who is often cast in the role of a tough criminal. Every time another hummingbird approached any of the feeders, Rutger attacked the bird and chased it off.

After Stephanie heard Pat's story, she decided to have a little talk with Rutger. This is an example of what I mean when I say that anyone can communicate with animals. Stephanie had no formal training in animal communication, but she believed she could do it, so she did.

Remember in Chapter 10 how I emphasized that you must praise an animal to gain its trust and attention? Stephanie started her conversation with Rutger by telling him she realized that he was a 'macho, dominant kind of guy bird' and as such his job was to protect the weaker birds, not attack them. She sent the feisty little bird a picture of the hummingbird feeders and told him to pick one feeder to guard, and let the other hummingbirds share the remaining six. She was picturing this as well as saying it, and sending out the feelings of pride the little bird must have felt at being the cock o' the walk.

This must have made sense to the bird because, to Stephanie's amazement, Rutger complied with her request. She suddenly found she could communicate with the birds. She was so pleased and surprised at how simple it really was.

Things were peaceful in Stephanie's garden for a few weeks, then a new challenge was mounted by a bird Stephanie called Sly Stallone. Feeling very confident, Stephanie had the same talk with Sly, sending out the pictures and emotions to match her words, and she experienced the same positive results. He picked another feeder to guard, leaving Rutger and the other birds alone.

Finally, an unusually dominant female showed up. Stephanie dubbed her Elizabeth Taylor and gave her the talk, and Liz picked a third feeder to guard. Things are currently peaceful but Stephanie has decided that if any more dominant birds show up, she's going to have to start buying nectar feeders wholesale.

Zula

One of my clients, Paula, a great animal lover, was living on a ranch on Galveston Island, where she was feeding and caring for a number of domestic, wild and feral animals. At the time she called, Paula was in the process of training a possum named Sowelu, whose mother had been killed. When the training was complete, Paula was to release Sowelu in the wild. But the raccoons on the ranch were so fierce that Paula found she couldn't release Sowelu and the possum ended up living in the house like a cat.

Though Paula was phoning about her missing cat, Zula, I connected first to Sowelu who was quite chatty. She told me that one night when she walked about the floor one of the cats had scratched her on the nose. Paula confirmed this had happened. Sowelu then told me she was confused about where Paula wanted her to go to the bathroom. When I asked Paula, she said she wanted the possum to use the litter box just like the cats. Paula said from that time forward, the possum never missed the litter box again. Then Sowelu complained that Paula had cleaned the floor under her bed with something that smelled horrible. When I asked Paula, she laughed and said she had been using a pine-scented cleanser, another example of how something chemical which may smell quite pleasant to humans can upset the sensitive noses of our animal friends, who like natural and not artificial odours.

There was a strong strain of Maine Coon Cat running among the feral cats on the ranch. Paula had adopted two females, Sylphan and Keffie, and a male she named Zula, a magnificent specimen of a Mackerel Coon Cat, who had an apricot underbelly to set off his distinctive raccoon-like markings. Though still somewhat feral, Zula had become a delightful companion for Paula, always clowning and making funny faces and lying about the house in a variety of unusual positions. It especially amused Paula when Zula fell asleep on his back with all four paws in the air. His sudden disappearance broke Paula's heart.

Sylphan came through next and informed me that she was a very clever cat with an exceptionally beautiful tail, and confessed it was she who had scratched Sowelu. Then she told me Keffie had a terrible pain in her back and could hardly walk. Paula confirmed this, too, and told me Keffie had been ill with a variety of complaints for some time.

I connected with Keffie and told Paula she had a pinched nerve in her back which could be helped with absent healing. I sent healing energy to Keffie and knew that my guides had relieved her pain.

But now my worry was Zula. Paula had searched the ranch with no luck. I relaxed, waited quietly and suddenly connected with a cat who told me he had once fallen into the water and had to swim hard to keep from drowning. When I told Paula she became very excited and said, 'We've got him!' because Zula, who was given to parading up and down railings, had once fallen from a rail into the canal which ran near the ranch house. We knew then that he was alive.

I asked Zula what had happened that caused him to leave the ranch. He said he had been fighting off the raccoons by standing on the rear verandah and hitting them on the head. Then two of the raccoons charged the verandah and he ran through the sliding glass door into the house, with the raccoons in hot pursuit. He told me the raccoons were really angry by then and he was afraid of their wrath. Raccoons have sharp claws and teeth which they won't hesitate to use in a fight, so Zula was right to be concerned about his safety, especially as he had provoked them.

Paula told me Zula knew he should leave the raccoons alone and was surprised to hear he had been teasing them. She provided plenty of food for both her cats and the raccoons so it shouldn't have been an issue of fighting over the food. But Zula told me he had told the raccoons to clear off because this was his house and his territory, and he didn't like sharing it with them.

Zula told me the raccoons chased him through Paula's kitchen, out through the cat flap and down the front verandah stairs. They kept on chasing him and he was frightened so he hadn't stopped running until he was off the ranch. I asked Zula which way he went and he sent me a picture of turning left as he went away from the ranch. That made sense to Paula who told me there was only one way to leave the ranch; you couldn't go north because of the water, and the road went south. That was where Zula had gone.

I asked Zula for any unusual landmarks he might have seen and he transmitted a picture of several houses. The most distinctive one was a large house with a lighted tower that looked like a steeple. Paula knew exactly where this house was. Zula said he went past there and then through a field. Though I had never been to Galveston Island and was miles away at my office during these communications, Paula said the physical descriptions I was giving her were highly accurate. She said the field Zula mentioned led to a couple of developments, Kahala Beach and Indian Beach. Paula had already prepared flyers. Using the information I had received from Zula, Paula went to those locations and put her flyers out. She spoke to everyone she saw about her beloved cat.

Though Zula loved Paula, he was jealous of the attention she paid the raccoons and a bit afraid they would hurt him if he returned to the ranch. He liked it where he was, and planned to stay. I asked him for some more landmarks and he sent me a picture of a satellite dish. This was most helpful to Paula, who told me that such dishes were forbidden by deed restrictions in Kahala Beach, but not in Indian Beach. We were gradually narrowing down the field of search.

The next day, two workmen called from Indian Beach and told Paula they had seen Zula. She phoned me again and when I connected to Zula, he told me he had seen the men and that their truck was dark blue, which Paula said it was. She started leaving food for Zula on the beach at that location, and quickly discovered there was a large colony of feral cats living there. Paula started staying out late at night, sitting on a deck-chair on Indian Beach, hoping for some glimpse of her pet. Though she saw many cats, there was no sign of Zula.

The following week, Paula called to consult me again, distraught that she hadn't seen Zula. She wanted me to tell her once more about the landmarks. I described the scenery on the route from the ranch, including an old house and another outbuilding.

Then Zula sent me a picture of a brown tabby he really liked, liked so well in fact that he had taken her as a mate. There were two kittens with her, a white and grey, and a calico. He sent me a picture of the drainage culvert where he had found them looking for water. The mother cat and her babies were all feral.

When I told this to Paula, she thought I was way off track as Zula had been neutered. I told her it was still possible for Zula to desire the company of a female cat despite his operation, but she thought I was wrong about the mother cat and her kittens.

That evening Paula went to the beach to put out food. She sat in the deck-chair for a couple of hours, reading by flashlight and waiting for Zula to appear. Suddenly Paula felt intense energy at her shoulder. She turned and there was the brown tabby mother cat lying about a hundred yards off in the field with her two kittens, one calico and the other grey and white, just as Zula had said. From that time forward, the tabby let Paula see her all the time, but there was still no sign of Zula.

Then, just as suddenly, the mother cat stopped appearing. I told Paula that Zula had told the tabby to stop coming out to her. By this time, Paula was emotionally drained, and she questioned whether we really were in touch with Zula or not. I could see the pain and frustration in her face. I asked Zula to tell me something only Paula would know, and he confessed he used to relieve himself in the water bowl to keep the dogs and raccoons away. When I relayed this to Paula, she was elated, because Zula had done that. But she still wondered why he would never show himself to her. He told me he was afraid Paula would take him back to the ranch where the wild raccoons were, and he was happy where he was and did not want to be removed. That was why he told the mother cat to stop going out when Paula visited.

Paula's friend Annette saw Zula at night on more than one occasion, but Paula never did, even though they were sometimes down on the beach together. Zula would tell me what Paula was wearing when she came to the beach, so we knew he was watching her. I felt that was the oddest situation. Here was a cat who obviously loved his mistress, and she was crazy about him and mourned his absence to the point where she sat on a deserted beach every night hoping to see him. Yet he would not show himself. He told me what she wore, where she sat, who she talked to and what she said, but he could not be convinced to come out.

In time Paula reluctantly accepted the fact that the beautiful cat she had rescued from a feral life had freely chosen to return to that precarious existence. She still put out food, but the hope that she would get her pet back began to fade.

Then something changed. Paula moved to Houston, and

was unable to go every night to put out food and water. We were in the middle of a fierce drought. When I connected with Zula, he complained about Paula's absence and of being thirsty and hungry. I told him that Paula had moved far away, and encouraged him to end his stand-off and come forward. I told him he could bring his companion and her offspring, and they would have all the food and water they wanted, whenever they wanted. Zula said he would think about it, but emphasized he had to be free. He had lived as a feral cat before, and his freedom was the most important thing to him. He loved Paula very much but did not want to be shut in a house.

We are still in touch with Zula. Fortunately, the drought ended with the onset of the tropical storm season, so Zula and his family are no longer thirsty. But they still live a dangerous and uncertain life. Paula is planning to move back to Galveston soon, and it is my feeling that when she moves into her new house, Zula will return to her, secure in the knowledge that he will not have to deal with the raccoons any more, and his desire for freedom will be respected.

These stories show how telepathic communication can be used to establish a link with either wild or feral animals. You do not have to have any special training, just an open mind. Anyone can use the techniques outlined in Chapter 10 to establish better communication with animals, whether wild or domestic.

Once you have learned to establish this special bond, the

hardest thing is learning how to let go. But there comes a time when every animal dies. That is what I discuss in the next chapter: how to cope when a beloved pet passes on to the next dimension.

CHAPTER 12

Fond farewells:
how to cope when a beloved pet dies

Perhaps the most difficult time I ever lived through was the illness and death of my beloved Rhodesian Ridgeback, Bella. I had her from a small puppy and over the years she had become my most constant companion.

For all of us who share our lives with pets, the time comes when we must say goodbye. No one likes to think about their pet dying, but since few animals other than parrots and tortoises have a life span comparable to that of humans, the day of grief is inevitable.

Domestic dogs and cats live an average of just ten to fifteen years, so during the course of our lives we may have to say goodbye over and over again, first to one beloved animal companion, then to another. I know from experience the pain does not lessen with repetition. Each time we lose a pet, we feel the sadness intensely.

But we must let our animal companions go when their time comes. The greatest gift we can give a dying pet is to send them on their way with our love and blessing so that they may make the transition from this earthly plane with dignity and at peace. If our grief at the thought of their death and our fear of what life will be like without them are so unmanageable that we cannot let our pets go, we cause animals who are in horrible pain to hang on and on, just to please us. That is a terribly irresponsible and unfeeling thing to do.

While I am speaking of responsibility, I want to remind you to be sure to make arrangements for your pet's ongoing care in case you yourself should precede your animal companion in death. I know of many pets who have been tossed out on the street by unfeeling relatives, or taken to non-humane shelters or pounds to be killed after their loving owner has passed on.

If you can, make arrangements with a reliable friend with whom your pet already has a loving relationship. Ask if they will take your pet in the event of your death. If your finances permit, leave a bequest to provide for your pet's care. Do this even if you are young and in perfect health, because none of us knows with any certainty the exact day and method of our own passing. If you walk out the door and get hit by a car today, your beloved pet could be hungrily wandering the streets or sitting in a cage at the pound tomorrow.

Death is a natural part of life, but sometimes we lose track of that. You must remember animals do not share our human fear of death; what they do fear is causing their owners pain when they depart. That is why they will struggle to hide an illness or injury, to save us from worry, and why a dog or cat approaching the end of its life will often take itself off into the woods. They choose to go back into the comforting embrace of nature to die, to spare their humans the agony of watching their passing.

Perhaps it would be helpful if I told you a little about where animals go when they die. Despite what some people are taught, I know animals are spiritual beings. When they

die, they do not go off into a void, into nothingness. They
go to a place of unearthly beauty, where joy, peace and
happiness reign supreme; where memories of pain, care
and worries fade into bliss. Knowing this helped me cope
when Bella passed over.

When I realized Bella was becoming ill, I connected to
her energy and got a feeling of pain in one of my legs. I
sensed she had a tumour, and our vet confirmed this.
Though I wanted to believe this would be one of my
miracle stories, deep inside I knew it was Bella's time to
go.

For weeks after I learned of Bella's illness, I gave her
healing, relieving the pain in her leg and praying that what
I knew to be true would not actually come to pass. I could
not yet let her go.

Finally, Bella's suffering became too much for me to bear.
I asked her if she wanted to go. Though she did not want
to leave her family, she said she was ready.

Fitz and Emma and I were heartbroken. I phoned my
sons in England, Sean and Patrick, to let them know that
Bella's time for leaving us was close. I didn't want my Bella
to experience the upset of going to the animal hospital,
which she didn't like, so I asked the vet to come to the
house so we could all be with her. That way, Bella would
be in her home surrounded by her loving family when she
left her physical body.

Though I felt tremendous sadness, I knew she would go
to a beautiful dimension where she would be happy and
free from pain.

Then I told Bella what was going to happen. I told her
we would see each other again. I asked her if she would

help me in my work with the animals when she passed over. She said she would. (And she does. I see her often and feel her presence while I am working.)

The evening came much too quickly. We all sat together on the floor with Bella: my husband Fitz and I, my daughter Emma, and Wellington and Foxy, too. I held her beautiful head in my lap, and we gave her permission to leave, to go with our love and blessing. The vet administered a shot which caused Bella to go to sleep as I held her in my arms. I knew when she left her physical body.

Bella's pain was no more; she was at peace. But our pain had just begun. She had gone on and we had to learn to live without her, but I knew that her energy would be with me for ever. We would never get over the loss; we would just get used to living without her.

That is what I am still doing now – learning to live without Bella's physical presence. I miss her companionship, her compassion, the joy we shared at happy times together, her unfailing love during sad times. I miss the feel of her soft velvet coat, the lick of her tongue against my cheek or hand, the beauty and love shining from her eyes for all of us to see, her joyous bark, her paw that lifted each time she wanted attention, the comfort of her presence at night on the end of my bed, and the protection that she gave to me at all times. I miss my Bella.

I would like to share with you the poem my son Patrick sent to me from England after Bella passed over. It has comforted me greatly.

Bella's Eulogy
by Patrick James

When we lose a friend like Bella,
only passing time can make a difference
to the way that we all feel.

And when her loss hurts really hard,
by looking back and remembering, we can find the pleasure
that will help ease the pain and change our tears to
laughter and joy.

Bella was a friend like no other, and her loyalty had no
barriers.
The loving light in all our hearts is Bella
who is within each of us.

The love she had for our family was her life,
and our love for Bella was our greatest pleasure.

Though no animal can take the place of a pet who has passed on, very often the addition of a new pet to the household can ease your loss. In the course of my rescue work soon after Bella's death, my newest dog Honey came into our lives. I feel as if Bella sent her to us, so that she could look after us and we after her.

Often it helps tremendously if you adopt another animal. You may feel guilty about bringing another animal into your home; that is natural. But don't let your grief keep your home empty of an animal companion for too long. Shelters are full of orphaned animals desperate for loving homes. Remember, you are not trying to replace the animal you have lost; just looking for another animal you can love as much, but in a different way.

Some of you will be unable to adopt a new animal quickly as you are in mourning. But I can honestly say from experience that getting a new animal really is the best way of healing your grief. I still miss Bella and think of her each day, but the presence of Foxy and Honey is a great comfort to me. When your pet is very ill, it is a true act of unselfish love to tell him it is okay for him to pass over and go. You will be doing your pet a great kindness if you can find the courage to do this.

If you are having trouble gathering your strength, just put yourself in your pet's body. Be aware of his physical pain and try to understand how it would feel if it was you. You go out to work daily, or to the cinema or a restaurant in the evening. You exercise at a gym and continue with the enjoyable activities of your daily life. We are busy and occupied and time passes quickly. But your sick pet can no longer play ball. He is no longer able to go for his walks. He can't enjoy his food. Time goes slowly for him as time does when we are unhappy and in pain. If you are allowing your pet to live in pain and suffering, ask yourself why. Is it for the few hours or few minutes a day you spend with him? The rest of the time you are off pursuing your activities, with your body fit and well and your mind occupied, while his days are long and filled with pain. This is not the way to love your pet. Do him a great kindness and let him go.

I had one client who brought me her very old cat, who was almost twenty and suffering from a variety of health problems. When I connected to the cat's energy, I discovered he was terribly anxious to pass over, but was hanging on because his owner was so adamant about not letting him go. The cat was in a great deal of pain, and I sent him some healing to relieve the pain, then decided to speak to his owner. But she had made up her mind the cat was going to stay no matter what.

I continued to work with her for a few weeks, doing what I could to help the cat, whose body was almost totally broken down. I felt very sorry for my client as she was not able to see past her own feelings. I felt even sorrier for her cat, who was trying desperately to hang on for his owner's sake. He was ready to go. I explained to her that it was time for her pet to pass over to the next dimension, and that she would be doing him a great kindness to let him go. I told her there was no more that I could do for her or for her pet. It was a decision she would have to make.

But there *are* some animals whose time hasn't come yet. There are many animals that vets have recommended for euthanasia who are walking around happy and healthy because their owners believed they could recover and refused to give up.

You must make the decision whether or not to let your pet go according to the information that is available to you at the time, and the best judgment of the vets who are caring for your animal. The very best way to make such a difficult decision is to trust your heart and your intuition, and do whatever they tell you to do. You will have a gut feeling in any case, and following that feeling will not steer you wrong.

If you feel your pet's life should be ended, go with that feeling. Make the decision and stick with it. Do not berate yourself or allow yourself to be eaten up with guilt if you must have an animal put down.

If you think there is a chance for recovery, go with that. You can always change your mind if your animal's condition deteriorates significantly. The important thing is not to let anyone else make this decision for you.

Of course we all hope our pets will die naturally. But sometimes it is not so easy. We have to take responsibility for our animal friends, and sometimes, when they are lingering in pain, we have to make the heart-wrenching decision to end their lives humanely so that we may also end their suffering.

The question of burial is a matter of individual choice. Some of you will prefer to have your animal buried on your property. Others prefer cremation of their pet's remains so they can carry the ashes with them in case they move.

One thing I do recommend is to find a sympathetic vet who will come to your home to put your pet to sleep in its familiar surroundings. If your vet will not do this, keep searching until you find one who will. It really helped me deal with Bella's passing to know that she died in her home, surrounded by the family she loved; the family that loved her in return.

I still see my Bella. Often when I walk Foxy and Honey on the nearby golf course, I can feel Bella's energy and see her running with my dogs. Her spirit is always present. I feel it very strongly.

Life is energy. On a spiritual level I know that energy can never be destroyed; it can only be transformed. Einstein was quoted as saying he believed in an afterlife for this very reason: that energy never dies. So I know that Bella has not truly left us; we just cannot see her physical body except in our minds. But I feel her, I sense and know she is there, still chasing after the squirrels and the birds, running towards the lake with Foxy and Honey and taking her morning swim.

There are times when Foxy feels Bella's presence too, and knows she is with us. I feel my love for her and know that no one can take away what I shared with my special friend: the happiness, the memories, the joy and love. My life and the lives of all my family have been richer because we were able to share Bella's life.

We now look forward to sharing our lives with another Ridgeback. One of my clients in Arizona, Anne, phoned to say she would like to give me a puppy from her next litter.

Bella would like to come back as a Ridgeback puppy, but for now she is working to help me on the other side. Bella is very happy with the work she is doing, helping other animals make the transition from this earthly plane to the spiritual realm.

My friend Karen had a little kitten that passed over, and when I asked Bella about it, Bella showed me a lovely picture of herself, swimming across the healing waters that animals pass through, with the kitten on her back. As soon as the kitten was no longer frightened, Bella gently rolled it into the water and it swam to the golden shore by itself, where angels were waiting to take the kitten to the spiritual realm.

After animals pass over, they rest for a while, just like humans. Then they have a decision to make, whether or not they want to stay where they are, or reincarnate and go back to the earth in another form to learn more. Occasionally, as Bella has indicated she will do, they may choose to come back in the same form again, but that is unusual.

I believe humans who are particularly sympathetic to animals have inhabited a variety of animal bodies in their previous lives, so they know the difficulties animals must go through as they make their way in this world, and devote themselves to easing those difficulties whenever they can.

I am unable to tell you how to make your pain go away when your pet is no longer sharing your physical life, or how to cope with your grief. No one else can know how you feel or cry your tears for you. That is an essential part of your recovery, to embrace the feelings of sorrow that you have. It may help to talk to people who understand about the love you had for your animal. The best support you can have is from others who have worked through their own loss. Sadly, many people do not feel about animals as we do, so be sure to find someone who does. Then you can pour your heart out.

You can't rush through grief. As the weeks pass, you will start to get back into your routine, but follow your own pace. Each of us deals with grief in our own way. Some get on with life quicker than others. I can only tell you to be glad for what you have experienced and learned from sharing your life with your animal companion. Time does help. As I said before, we never entirely get over the loss . . . we just get used to living without them.

With an animal you may know a wonderful, close and loving relationship, and a richness and satisfaction you may never experience with another human being. The happy relationships we share with our pets are the jewels in our lives. All the material possessions in the world cannot equal this joy. Sharing love with your pet is one of life's sublime experiences. When human beings understand this, the planet will be a wonderful place for us all to live.

Many of you who read this book will have experienced the loss of a pet. I hope these few words will help you turn your sad memories into joyful ones. Remember this is not the end. Know that one day when our time comes to journey on to a higher dimension, you will be reunited with your loving pets once again.

How you can help animals in your everyday life

Hardly a day passes when I don't see some animal that could benefit from a little human assistance. There are so many unwanted animals, and so many die each year because of human neglect.

As much as I love animals, I lived for years in ignorance of the cruelty they were subject to. In fact, when I heard stories of cruelty to animals, I turned away. I didn't want to hear such awful things; they sickened me. My eldest son, Sean James, inherited my love of animals and went to work for the Royal Society for the Prevention of Cruelty to Animals (RSPCA) in London while still a teenager. Though I was proud of him, I made it clear I didn't want to hear any sad stories, for when I listened, I couldn't get to sleep that night. I couldn't get the horrifying pictures of cruelty out of my mind.

This was during the time I had shut myself off from the world of animal communication, so I was living in a sort of ignorant bliss. I didn't realize how important it was for people who love animals to support animal rights and vigorously oppose the cruel treatment of animals for any reason.

I was working as a fashion model in England, and often had the chance to buy the clothes I modelled at very good prices. I fell in love with a beautiful lynx jacket I modelled at Harvey Nichols, and bought it to wear on a ski trip to the Alps. I wore the jacket for three years in a state of perfect enjoyment, completely unaware of how many animals had sacrificed their lives for this garment.

One afternoon, I was having my tea in our drawing room. I put on the television and sat down to pour. When I looked up, there was a beautiful lynx walking gracefully across the snow. I thought what a magnificent creature he was. Then, to my horror, his leg was caught in a cruel trap which mangled his paw. The pain must have been excruciating. Unable to eat, drink or move, the lynx was trapped in agony for four days before the hunters returned to check their traps. He began to chew off his own leg in a desperate effort to escape. When the hunter finally approached the lynx, his gun aimed at the cat's head, I could see the relief in the poor animal's eyes. He understood the horrendous torture would soon be over.

The full realization of how many animals had suffered for me to be able to wear my lynx jacket hit me with the force of a thunderbolt. Tears streaming down my face, I took my jacket, walked into my garden, poured lighter fluid on it and set it on fire. From that day forward, I have never worn another animal pelt on my body.

That event raised my conscience concerning animal welfare, and since then I have worked for the good of animals, a mission that has culminated in the work I am doing today. Now I would like to enlist your help in the fight.

First, you must take responsibility for the animals that are in your care. Treat them with love, kindness and respect, for they are God's creatures and put here for us to care for, not to exploit. Feed them, play with them and protect them. Have them spayed or neutered to keep from adding to the pet overpopulation problem. Provide proper veterinary care. Give generously of your affection and attention, for animals thrive on this.

Most of us have to go out to work every day, leaving our pets unattended. Long gone is the notion of the housewife at home – as you will have seen from my stories, many of my clients are working women. But I believe we need to think of pet care in the same way as we plan for child care – and as with child care, the variety of solutions ranges from family, neighbours and friends to professionals.

A pet sitter does not stay in your home all day, but visits perhaps twice a day to feed your pet, and where necessary (particularly in the case of dogs), exercise the animal briefly in your garden or around the neighbourhood. Alternatively, you might want to consider placing your animal in a kennel when you are out, although most people only do this when away for several days, and sometimes your pet's age, health or temperament means this is not a viable option. Vets will often recommend pet sitters to their clients if they think the animal will benefit from such an arrangement, and may even provide a list of sitters in the area. In my experience many sitters are retired people, and can not only provide references but insurance documentation.

The pressures of a job and career, a marriage and raising a family require a great deal of organization for all of us; this must also extend to our pets. My hope is that with awareness of pet care problems answers will evolve, and just as we co-operate in car pools and school buses, we will provide adequate care for the animals who share their lives with us.

Don't crop your dog's tail or ears, or declaw your cat. These are cruel and unnecessary procedures, relating more to human whim and laziness than any need of the animal. Cats, in particular, suffer when they are declawed. It would be like having your fingernails pulled out, one by one. They are left with no way to defend themselves and often resort to biting instead.

If you see an animal being neglected or mistreated, have the courage to do something about it. You do not have to place yourself in danger. Sometimes a phone call to the appropriate agency is enough to rescue an animal in distress. If you can help a neighbour who isn't able to care for a pet but still wants their love and companionship, do so.

Take in lost and stray animals and do your best to reunite them with their owners. Join an animal welfare organization and volunteer your time. Such groups can always use extra help.

Do not support organizations which profit from animal exploitation or cruelty, such as rodeos and circuses. Do not buy products which use cruel and unnecessary animal testing. Don't wear fur. Fake fur today is almost indistinguishable from the real thing, so if you want the look of fur, opt for the fabulous fake instead and save an animal from suffering and dying in some inhumane trap.

If you are taking Hormone Replacement Therapy (HRT), make sure your prescription derives from a plant source. The oestrogen for these preparations is sometimes extracted from the urine of pregnant mares that spend their eleven-month pregnancies standing chained in tiny stalls, without even the room to lie down. Can you imagine never being able to lie down or rest even once during the whole of a pregnancy? As soon as the foals are weaned, they are sold for meat. Then the mares are impregnated and chained up again and again, until they can no longer reproduce, at which time they follow their foals to the slaughterhouse.

If we all take just a bit of responsibility on our own shoulders, we could do much to reduce the suffering of animals and make this world a better place for humans and animals alike.

Please help.

About the Authors

Sonya 'Sunny' Fitzpatrick was born in the Midlands in a quiet rural area where she acquired a deep love for all animals. At the age of seventeen, Sonya left home to pursue a career in fashion and modelling in London. During this period she worked in all the major fashion capitals of Europe, appeared frequently on television, and modelled for many noted designers, including Norman Hartnell, couturier to the Queen.

Sonya moved to Houston in 1991 to establish an etiquette business. She is a consultant to several major corporations, including Continental Airlines, and many of Houston's most prominent families in matters of social and business etiquette.

As an animal communicator, she is a regular guest on phone-in radio talk shows in Houston and Dallas, where she helps countless people solve their pet problems. Her clientele has expanded to include animal lovers from all over the world, who consult her regularly concerning health and behavioural problems with their pets. She is also a popular speaker and regularly gives seminars on animal behaviour and healing. In 1996, Sonya was featured in a television documentary film exploring the relationship between man and animals.

Patricia Burkhart Smith is a journalist whose work has won fifteen awards since 1988; five from the Louisiana Press Association and ten from the Texas Community Newspaper Association (TCNA). Her weekly humour column, 'Half Sweet, Half Acid,' was voted the best original column of 1995 by TCNA, and has won an award at the state level each of the past three years.

Smith, the author of four published books and numerous newspaper and magazine articles, has also hosted her own radio show and been regularly featured as a humourist on an award-winning local cable access show in Texas.

Smith is currently a self-employed freelance writer who writes and edits for diverse business clients. She is also the proud mother of two children, and shares her home with three cats and a turtle.

A few letters I have received

From a vet:
I have been involved with alternative medicine for over eight years, utilizing these methods in conjunction with traditional Western medicine. My path crossed with Sonya when I was treating Desert Vision, an Arab stallion, and a very accomplished endurance rider. As I was checking the acupuncture points on his back his owner mentioned the areas that she thought were affected, and they correlated exactly with my diagnosis. I was literally stunned when she told me she had learned this from an animal communicator who had been told by Desert Vision where his problems were!

While working on Voyager, a quarterhorse gelding used for trail riding, it always seemed that he preferred acupuncture treatment to the chiropractic manipulations. His owner agreed — Sonya had told her!

As a veterinarian, I have developed a deep empathy for the creatures that I minister to. The results of this bond, both on a personal and medical level, has helped my patients. Their communications with Sonya have concurred with my theories of treatment modalities, and reinforced in my mind not only the healing potential of what I do, but the insight and compassion of Sonya.

Dear Sunny,

We cannot express that we are beyond gratitude for your healing of our cat Windy. You might remember that in leaping off our bed, she slammed her head against the wall and developed a severe concussion. This caused complications that then lead to pneumonia. Since she was near death, and having done everything possible at home, we were forced to take her to the emergency clinic.

As her medical records show, Windy was having Grand Mal seizures, periodic stoppage of breathing and other near-death signs. The clinic called more than five times to say that Windy appeared to have died. But here's where the miracles began to appear to be at work. We are so lucky that we were able to reach you every time Windy appeared to have died, or her lifesigns slipped away. Each time, you called her back into her body. This never failed to amaze all the doctors as well as the staff.

Then something humorous happened. You recounted things that Windy told you were being said about her at the clinic. When we mentioned these to the doctors and the staff, they were confounded. 'How', they asked, 'did you know what we said?' When we said that our cat, who was after all comatose at the time and for all practical purposes dead, had told you and that you then told us, you should have seen their expressions! They knew what we were saying was true, but it certainly went against all conventional medical training.

I should say that the emergency staff gradually began to accept your admonitions that animals are intelligent, can comprehend, and that the delicate balance between life and death is often affected by what they hear. By consequence, the co-operation of the entire medical team became quite extraordinary. In fact, on our next visit we found a sign attached to Windy's oxygen chamber that read, 'Speak and think only positive thoughts around Windy!'

All we can say is that it was your communication and healing that made the difference. Through communication, Windy learned to focus on and respond to your higher healing. Today, she is known as a medical miracle that has transcended the impossible.

We thank you.

Dave, Alanna and Windy

Dearest Sonya,

Miracles do happen! You brought my precious little dog Sugar, who had gone missing, back to us. We had heard about you through a friend, and due to the importance of timing, you fitted me into your busy schedule. Looking at a picture of Sugar, you immediately began to communicate with her, telling me things that no one else would know, and exact in details of different aspects of our lives that only Sugar could know. I cannot describe to you the incredible feeling it was to know that my dog was well and communicating with you. Through much prayer, talking to Sugar and some specific advice from you, my mission to find my dog continued along a different avenue, and I believe it was by following the prayer instructions of one of your psychic helpers that we were able to change one man's heart, so that my baby Sugar was indeed returned to me. I pray now that others too can experience her miraculous talent!

With much love and gratitude,

Catherine

Dearest Sonya,

I wanted to thank you and to update you on Lexus the beagle's status. The last time we spoke, it was by telephone and I was at the vet's office. Little Lexus had just had surgery, and you promised to send one of your colleagues to be with her through the night. Lexus came through with flying colours, and is home and happy now, and, I think, set to win a few more rosettes!

But let me fill you in on the details of the part *you* played in this. I had been to see you about Lexus, a prize-winner, two weeks before. The problem was that she wasn't holding her tail up in the show ring. You immediately said, 'Lexus is confused,' and kept saying that, over and over again. And how right you were.

You also said, 'Lexus says she has been having a bad time of it lately. She says what with her leg hurting, and everything else . . .' And at the very end of our session, you said, 'Lexus says she has to urinate a lot. It feels like she has to go all the time.' I then told you I'd taken her to the vet about this, and you counselled me to take her back again.

Well, I didn't. But about ten days later Lexus suddenly 'crashed', as the medics say. I came home from work and she didn't wag her tail, just looked very worried. She didn't eat, and suddenly she couldn't hold her head up. She couldn't place her feet under her normally, and she walked in a crouch. I called a friend for help, and by the time she got there Lexus had collapsed, with dilated pupils, unresponsive to light. I was sure she was dying. My friend rushed her to her employer's vet clinic and they started an IV line with, I am sure, only seconds to spare.

Lexus started coming round nicely with the introduction of intravenous fluids, and she spent the night in an emergency clinic. It turned out she has a birth defect: hundreds of extra blood vessels carry her blood from the intestines directly to the heart, instead of through her liver where it can be filtered and detoxified. This led to ammonia crystals in her urine, which made her need to urinate all the time, as you saw. It also allowed toxic compounds to circulate freely in her blood, including into her brain, leading to intense mental confusion and disorientation, as you kept repeating.

Unfortunately, Lexus' problem cannot be fixed surgically. She can, however, be treated with a special diet and with certain drugs. We hope to have Lexus with us at least three or four years more, with God's good grace.

Oddly enough, Lexus' litter sister, Seville, has the very same thing and was diagnosed the same week as Lexus. And I have a third dog who may have it too — she is due for diagnostic imaging tests in two weeks.

Although it is hard to think they may have a seriously shortened lifespan (Lexus and Seville are not a yet a year and a half old, and Flossie is ten months), I am grateful for whatever months, weeks, even days, of life they have. And the change in Lexus is so very dramatic! Now that her condition is being treated, she wags her tail, jumps and plays with the other dogs, barks, and is completely back to her happy former self. Seville and Flossie have not shown any symptoms.

I just wanted to let you know how completely accurate your readings were, and to thank you, so very much, for your prayers and interventions on her behalf the day of her

surgery. I am sure I will be seeing you in the future. And I will buy your book, because I know I'll love it!
Take good care,
Margaret

To whom it may concern:
My business, Creature Comforts, is such that I am in constant contact with animals. Our service involves their care in the comfort of their own homes, in the absence of their owners. As you might suspect, being able to communicate clearly with my 'animal kingdom clients' would be an invaluable asset during times when their needs could not be adequately conveyed via conventional means.

Sonya Fitzpatrick has been an incredible help to me, not only in clearing up communications with my own animals, but also with some that have been left in my care while their owners are away. She has also been very helpful with my daughter's dog, Amadeus, who is currently in training with the Houston Flyball Association. He was exhibiting very aggressive behaviour toward the other dogs on his team, and was in danger of being excluded from competition. Through Sonya's efforts, we were able to determine his fear of being tugged with the leash – a method of control that had been used in a very abusive way before he became a cruelty confiscation by the HSPCA – and reassure him that he was in no danger. He is now competing successfully without incident.

Sonya was also instrumental in assisting my dog Rusty in overcoming a chronic ear infection. Without any input from me whatsoever, Sonya communicated with her and learned that she missed a yard nearby our previous home that had a gate where she used to sit and watch the squirrels. Rusty also told Sonya that there was a chair in the house where we live now that she liked in particular, and she didn't like sharing it with the other dogs. Both statements were absolutely accurate. Sonya then sent Rusty some healing messages, and her infection began to clear up almost immediately.

Sonya's genuine concern for the animals in her care, coupled with her spiritual insight, are of great value to anyone who lives and/or works with our beloved members of the animal kingdom.
Sharon Carter, Creature Comforts

Dear Sonya,
Thank you for telling me what to do to cure my turtle of his illness. After you told me to move its aquarium back to its former location, change to a larger enclosure and make the water much deeper, add pebbles, a green plant and a small fish, and filtrate the water, I decided to do all those things. But to be honest, I just believed it was probably a waste of money because I thought the turtle would die. It hadn't eaten in seven days and was very sick and lethargic, spewing mucus from its nostrils even though I had been administering antibiotics.

Within two days, the turtle seemed somewhat revived, although he was still not eating. Today, six days after I made the changes you suggested, the turtle's appetite is voracious, he is swimming and diving for the first time. He and the fish seem quite companionable, as you suggested, although the pet store insisted the turtle would eat the fish! [But read Pat's story in Chapter Seven . . .]

A few days after I made the changes you suggested, I happened to read a book on turtle maintenance. The exact habitat conditions you suggested were outlined as being mandatory for my species of turtle, a red-eared slider. The book goes so far as to say that if you cannot provide these conditions, do not try to maintain a red-eared slider!

I am amazed because first, you had no way of knowing I had moved the turtle's aquarium, and secondly, because you did not know the species of turtle. Any other species would have continued to thrive in the habitat I provided, but the book said that after a red-eared slider gets to be a certain size, if it doesn't have deep water to swim in, it will not thrive!

Thank you again for your help.

Patricia B. Smith

Editor, *The Woodlands Villager*

TO CONTACT SONYA FITZPATRICK
please write to the following address:

395 Sawdust Road, Suite 2003
Houston, Texas 77380
United States of America

Index

adventure, sense of 130
affection, displays of 100
aggressive behaviour 31, 35–6,
    37, 43–4, 45–8, 49, 73–8
allergies 119
American Veterinary
    Association 52
angel guides 7, 29, 102, 103–4,
    105, 107–8, 109–10
    see also healing
Animal Control 143
animal shelters 133, 137, 155, 158,
    201–2
animal welfare 208–12
attention, quality 41
attention-seeking behaviour
    37, 39, 40–1, 53, 76
attention span 173–4

balance of nature 185–6
Battersea Dogs Home 155
bees 10–11
Beverly (client) 122–3

body language 37–8, 173
breeds, varying temperaments
    of 98
Burkhart Smith, Patricia vii,
    113–17, 158, 173, 177–87,
    214

calming technique 145
Carol (SF's friend) 78–80
cat lovers 132, 158
cats
    communication technique
    170
    curiosity of 129
    declawing 41–2, 211
    energy-reading and
    tracking skills 125–6, 132
    furniture-scratching 41–2,
    72, 73, 98–9
    intolerant of ill treatment
    124
    life span 197